D0911650

BUSTED

An Illustrated History of Drug Prohibition in Canada

BUSTED

An Illustrated History of
Drug Prohibition in Canada

Susan Boyd

FERNWOOD PUBLISHING
HALIFAX & WINNIPEG

Editing: Curran Faris
Cover design: Mike Carroll
Interior design: David Lester

Printed and bound in Canada

Published by Fernwood Publishing
32 Oceanvista Lane, Black Point, Nova Scotia, B0J 1B0
and 748 Broadway Avenue, Winnipeg, Manitoba, R3G 0X3
www.fernwoodpublishing.ca

Fernwood Publishing Company Limited gratefully acknowledges the financial support of the Government of Canada, the Manitoba Department of Culture, Heritage and Tourism under the Manitoba Publishers Marketing Assistance Program and the Province of Manitoba, through the Book Publishing Tax Credit, for our publishing program. We are pleased to work in partnership with the Province of Nova Scotia to develop and promote our creative industries for the benefit of all Nova Scotians. We acknowledge the support of the Canada Council for the Arts, which last year invested $153 million to bring the arts to Canadians throughout the country.

Library and Archives Canada Cataloguing in Publication

Boyd, Susan C., 1953-, author
Busted: an illustrated history of drug prohibition in
Canada / Susan Boyd.

Includes bibliographical references and index.
ISBN 978-1-55266-976-1 (softcover)

1. Drug control—Canada—History. 2. Drug abuse—
Canada—Pictorial works. I. Title.

HV5840.C3B685 2017   362.290971   C2017-903103-1

Contents

Acknowledgements

IN 2000, THE BRILLIANT RESTORATIVE JUSTICE SCHOLAR AND ACTIVIST DENNIS Sullivan encouraged me to explore and write about the history of the regulation of altered states of consciousness and the resistance to it. I have been doing so ever since. In 2004, Dave Diewert and Bud Osborn, long-time social justice activists, founded Creative Resistance in Vancouver. The grassroots group called for an end to drug prohibition. I joined in with them alongside other activists. For many years, we set up public forums in Vancouver to provide a space for people to talk about the harms of, and alternatives to, prohibition. With Dave Diewert in charge of the logistics, sound system, introduction and discussion period, Bud Osborn recited his exquisite poetry, Mark Haden discussed alternative legal frameworks for drug regulation and Clinton Sherman eloquently challenged negative stereotypes about people who use heroin. I often presented a PowerPoint that visually illustrated the history of drug prohibition in Canada. This led to the genesis of this book. I owe a debt of gratitude to Creative Resistance and Dennis Sullivan.

I would also like to thank Fernwood Publishing for their support in the publication of *Busted*. Without their support the book would not have been published. Special thanks to Errol Sharpe, Wayne Antony, Curran Faris, Brenda Conroy and Beverley Rach for making this book happen. Wayne was especially helpful and endured reading and editing several copies of the manuscript before the final one was completed. I would also like to thank David Lester for his creative expertise and the beautiful design and layout of *Busted*.

Many people and institutions provided photos, images and copyright permission to reproduce the images in the book. I would like to thank AQPSUD, AAWEAR, John Bonner, Canadian Drug Policy Coalition, B.C. Compassion Club Society, Canadian HIV/AIDS Legal Network, Dr. Peter Centre, DUAL, Iain Mitchell-Boyd, John Donoahue, Marc Emery, Jodie Emery, Hugh Gibson, Mark Haden, International Centre for Science in Drug Policy, L'Injecteur, David Malmo-Levine, MAPS Canada, Bob Masse, Kent Monkman, REDUN, Henri Robideau, SNAP, David South, Richard Tetrault, Vancouver Area Network of Drug Users, WAHRS, and Nettie Wild. Thanks also to Archive of Jesuits in Canada and Michael Metosage, Archives of Ontario, Canadian Museum of History, Canadian Press, City of Edmonton Archives, City of Vancouver Archives, Flickr, Écomusée du fier monde, *Georgia Straight*, Health Canada, Hudson's Bay Company Archives, Archives of Manitoba, Infomart and *Saskatoon Star Phoenix*, Library and Archives Canada, U.S. Library of Congress, Provincial Archives of Saskatchewan, *The Province*, National Geographic Creative, National Film Board of Canada, National Maritime Museum, NATOPA, New Westminster Museum and Archives, Ontario, Ministry of Government and Consumer Services, Pacific Newspaper Group, Pacific Tribune Collection, Sears Canada, Photofest, Sun & Province Infoline, Textile Museum of Canada, Time Inc., *Toronto Star*, Getty Images, Toronto Public Library, UBC Museum of Anthropology, United Church of Canada, United Nations Photo Library, UBC Library, U.S. National Library of Medicine, Vancouver Area Network of Drug Users (VANDU), Vancouver Police Museum, Vancouver Public Library, and Wellcome Library. I would also like to thank the University of Victoria for their support.

I would also like to thank a number of people who provided me with information, Lynne Belle-Isle, John Conroy, Sheila Lacroix, Craig Heron, Alex Sherstobitoff, David Malmo-Levine and Hilary Black. Thanks to those who took the time to read over sections of the book and provided comments: Fernwood's external reviewers, Beth Abbott, Jade Boyd, Neil Boyd, Rielle Caplier, Dara Culhane, Patricia Erickson, Lenora Marcellus, Ron Abrahams, and Donald MacPherson. Any mistakes are of my own making.

For Bud and others
who have suffered under
drug prohibition

Criminalizing Drug Use

SINCE DRUG PROHIBITION WAS INTRODUCED TO CANADA OVER A CENTURY AGO, more than three million people have been arrested (busted) for a drug offence. Yet prohibition does not deter people from using criminalized drugs—these substances have become more desirable and visible in our everyday lives. Every day we see images of police rounding up suspected drug traffickers and people "shooting up" or smoking cannabis in films, TV series, YouTube and photographs in newspapers and online. Rock, rap and even pop songs praise cannabis and its effect. We often hear police and politicians expound on the evils of illegal drugs like heroin, cannabis, cocaine and methamphetamine, but at the same time, pharmaceutical companies cajole people about the benefits of similar, but legal, drugs like codeine, Marinol and Adderall. In Canada, even though the government claims that it will end cannabis prohibition by 2018, law enforcement is still arresting large numbers of people for cannabis possession, and the laws to incarcerate individuals for growing more than five cannabis plants have still not been repealed as this book goes to press. In some U.S. states, cannabis is legally regulated, and adults can buy, consume and grow up to five plants. We also see counter images of normalized cannabis use at events like 4/20 where citizens defy current federal law.

People use drugs for a variety of reasons, including pleasure, medicinal and spiritual use. For over a century, criminalized/illegal drugs have held our attention rather than diminishing in power. Given their prominence in our lives and in the media, it appears that our interest in these demonized drugs grows stronger with each passing decade. Our efforts to prohibit them in Canada are simply not a success.

This book is a short history of Canadian drug prohibition, the resistance to it and significant events that have shaped drug policy and practice. It is illustrated by visual reproductions from the late 1700s to the present, including photos, paintings, drawings, posters, book covers, film stills, official documents, newspaper articles and headlines that show significant moments in the history of drug prohibition and resistance to it in Canada.

Drug prohibition in Canada is a drug control system adopted in the early 1900s and expanded on for more than a century. In Canada, drug prohibition is primarily a criminal justice system approach. In the early 1900s, specific drugs, such as opium and cocaine, and the few people who used them, were deemed evil and criminal. Moral reformers (vocal individuals and groups that identify a "social problem" and then propose solutions which correspond with their own priorities) who champion drug prohibition claim that criminalization will lower consumption, addiction rates and drug trafficking. Thus, harsh drug laws were enacted with severe penalties. In the early twentieth century, drugs like opium were associated with Chinese men, who were depicted as foreign Others (outsiders to the white Christian nation) intent on corrupting moral white women and men. In the years to come, these negative stereotypes and myths were easily reactivated to inflame new drug scares and to support further prohibitionist policy. As much as anything else, Canada's drug laws are based on racial, class and gender prejudices and are aimed at controlling these groups of people. Drug prohibition has also been intricately tied up with colonization.

Negative stereotyping and visual representation in popular culture and news media also accompanied the criminalization of drugs. A century of law enforcement and media commentary linking drugs like heroin, cocaine and cannabis, and the people who use and sell them, to violence and crime supported harsh drug prohibitionist policies. Since the enactment of our first drug laws, the list of criminalized drugs has grown longer and the punishments more severe. Still, the goals of drug prohibition have not been met.

It is now well documented that prohibition has not stopped the use of drugs, but it has worsened the health and well-being of not only those who use them but also those who do not use them. Drug prohibition results in increased imprisonment, child apprehension and human rights violations. Moreover, prohibition undermines health services such as prevention and treatment services that effectively counter HIV and hepatitis C epidemics and drug overdose deaths. The harms stemming from drug prohibition are not limited to illegal drug users and traffickers: families and communities also bear the brunt of our drug policies. Drug prohibition is a multi-billion dollar experiment that has utterly failed.

In this book, the history of addiction is not fully explored. Other writers have tackled this concept. Yet, fear of addiction or the "addictive" qualities of some drugs have fueled drug scares in Canada. However, specific drugs do not compel people to use them, and most people do not experience problematic drug use or become dependent on the drugs that they use. Only a small percentage of drug use can be considered problematic and oftentimes it is situational rather than lifelong. I do not make light of the lives of people who experience problematic drug use or their suffering. But, we must acknowledge that there are "multiple trajectories into, within, and out of addiction"[1] and multiple experiences of non-problematic use. People's diverse experiences with drugs cannot be divorced from historical, social, cultural, psychological, biological, "political, legal and environmental contexts."[2] This book emphasizes that experiences and outcomes of drug use are shaped by one's social status and environment. People who use illegal drugs are subject to a host of discriminatory and punitive legal, social and medical regulation; however, the level of control and its impact are linked to social status—people from poor and marginalized communities are much more likely to be severely criminalized. Historically, and in contemporary times, some ideas about addiction promote social injustice.[3] Therefore, this book, in part, explores how people who use criminalized drugs have fought back against discrimination. Throughout drug prohibition history, people who use illegal drugs have been framed as immoral, criminal, pathological and out of control. People who are dependent on legal drugs, such as tobacco or alcohol, are slightly stigmatized in contemporary society, but they do not experience the same level of legal discriminatory practices directed at people who use illegal drugs.

Around the world, many citizens, and some governments, are turning away from discriminatory drug prohibitionist policies. Nations, states, provinces and cities are developing alternative drug policies based on reducing harm that work best for their citizens and their social, political, health and legal systems. Drug policy is rooted in local, national and international history, and drugs are defined and framed differently over time. Canadian drug policy is populated by moral reformers, activists, politicians, drug users, concerned citizens, law enforcement, health providers, Supreme Court judges, constitutional lawyers and plaintiffs.

On October 19, 2015, Canadians voted in a Liberal Federal Government that, in part, campaigned to end cannabis prohibition. In April 2017 the *Cannabis Act* was tabled in the House of Commons. It is too soon to know if the Act will become law. However, the Act, and preventable tragedies such as the opioid overdose crisis in Canada, has fuelled a heated debate about our drug policy. In order to chart the future, it is worthwhile for us as Canadians to know our history of prohibition.

NOTES

1. Reinarman, Craig, and Robert Granfield. 2015. "Addiction is not just a brain disease: Critical studies of addiction." In R. Granfield and C. Reinarman (Eds.), *Expanding Addiction: Critical Essays*. New York: Routledge.
2. Fraser, Suzanne. 2017. "The future of 'addiction': Critique and composition." *International Journal of Drug Policy*. 44: 130-134
3. Hart, Carl. 2017. "Viewing addiction as a brain disease promotes social injustice." *Nature Human Behaviour*. 1(0055): 1.

1

Plant Drugs and Colonization: 1800s and Earlier

Historically, people have used plant-based drugs for medicinal, cultural and spiritual use. Prior to the rise of the pharmaceutical industry in the 1800s, families relied on plants to reduce pain, to heal and to maintain health. Right up until the nineteenth century, there was little distinction between medical and non-medical use of plant-based drugs, and all classes of people consumed them. In fact, opium, alcohol and tobacco consumption were embedded in social custom in Britain and France.

Of course what was called the New World by white explorers and

Prince of Wales Fort, Hudson's Bay, engraved hand-coloured print by Samuel Hearne, 1797
(Library and Archives Canada, 1970-188-680 W.H. Coverdale Collection of Canadiana).

settlers in the 1500s was not empty. It was home to diverse Indigenous nations with their own forms of political systems, languages and social, cultural, health and spiritual practices. Indigenous people used a variety of plant-based medicines and foods that they introduced to early white settlers. Due to the diversity of Indigenous culture, geographical regions, plants, languages and traditions, their medicines, ceremonies and spiritual beliefs also differ. However, many contemporary Western medicines are derived from Indigenous medicines.

Alongside trading companies, Catholic missions were set up in the early 1600s in New France, and following the British Conquest of 1759–60, Protestant missions became more common. These trading posts, military forts and settlements built by the French and British settlers displaced longstanding Indigenous communities from their homelands. Traders, politicians, religious leaders, and moral reformers also used the Christianization of Indigenous peoples to justify colonization. Colonialism was driven by Western imperialism, the quest for new resources and lands, and it was supported by Western philosophies and eugenics, proponents of which argued that white Europeans were superior to all other races.

Painting by Frances Ann Hopkins, Voyageurs, 1869 (Library and Archives Canada, 1989-401-1).

ALCOHOL

Fur traders from New France, the Hudson's Bay Company (incorporated in 1670), and the North West Company (formed in 1780), as well as other British, French, and U.S. settlers brought their drug of choice—alcohol—along with their religions, laws and diseases with them upon settlement. All of this had devastating consequences for Indigenous peoples. The land (much of which is unceded) that is now considered to be part of the Canadian state was virtually alcohol free prior to colonization. White settlers introduced alcohol to Indigenous peoples, and trading posts sold and traded whisky for important trade items such as furs. Canada's first drug prohibition was directed at Indigenous peoples. In Canada, colonization played a significant role in the racialization of drug policy.

Drawing of Indigenous person trading for alcohol and (below) an altered state of consciousness. Created by an unknown Indigenous artist from the Pacific Northwest. Collected by Father Pierre-Jean De Smet, a Jesuit missionary, around 1847–48 (The Archive of the Jesuits in Canada and Michael Metosage).

Alcohol is one of our oldest drugs; it is made from fruits and grains,. Although not universally accepted as a legal beverage, it continues to be one of the most popular drugs around the world. In the 1700s, alcohol was embedded into Western culture, consumed for pleasure and medicinal purposes.

However, there was some opposition to alcohol, especially hard liquor, by Protestant clergy and upper-class moral reformers. Accompanying British imperialism and colonialism, the Protestant Christian mission movement emerged in England in the late 1700s. Devotees became active in setting up foreign missions to convert "uncivilized" and "heathen," "non-Christian" people, including Indigenous peoples, in Canada. After the Seven Years War, Britain, acquired Canada from France in 1763. As a result, more Protestant missions were established

Cartouche by William Faden of fur trade, 1777 (Library and Archives Canada).

in Canada. Adherents of the Christian mission movement were staunch temperance advocates. Distinguishing themselves from "uncivilized" and Catholic, lower-class people, Western Protestant missionaries and temperance advocates adopted religious dedication, sobriety and self-control as their template for middle- and upper-class respectability. As the temperance movement in Canada became more active in the early 1800s and 1900s, women were at the centre of this movement. Not having the federal vote until 1918, these women put their political energies into alcohol prohibition and other moral reform movements such as child saving. White middle- and upper-class reformers at this time regarded morality and sobriety as innate to women. They saw women as defenders of both home and nation. Rather than indict poverty, rapid urbanization, industrial capitalism and colonization for a wide array of social ills, they blamed alcohol. Furthermore, the conversion of Indigenous peoples to Western Christian religions, morals, and values, including sobriety, became a goal of temperance reformers.

The Tree of Temperance, coloured lithograph by Currier and Ives, 1872 (Wellcome Library, London).

Temperance supporters also sought to suppress the liquor trade between white traders and Indigenous people in Canada. Although federal alcohol prohibition had a short history in Canada in the early 1900s (see Chapter 5), it was imposed on Indigenous people for over a century.

Ontario Women's Christian Temperance Union, cloth banner, 1877 (Textile Museum of Canada).

Rejecting Indigenous sovereignty, the *Gradual Civilization Act* of 1857 and the *Gradual Enfranchisement Act* of 1869, which were consolidated into the *Indian Act* and passed in 1876 under the leadership of Prime Minister John A. Macdonald, regulated all aspects of life for those labelled "Status Indians" by the Canadian Government. Thus, Macdonald sought to consolidate and extend control over the lives of Indigenous peoples and nations. The Act is understood by many as an instrument of genocide imposed on Indigenous peoples. The Dominion of Canada was envisioned as a white, Christian nation by British colonists. Indigenous people, and later Chinese, Japanese and South Asian people, were seen as Outsiders to white nation building.

Notice of liquor law posted on telegraph pole in Bella Coola, B.C., by Harlan I. Smith, 1923 (photo Archives, Canadian Museum of History, 58543).

After Confederation, some provincial legislation banned the sale of alcohol to Indigenous people. For example, Nova Scotia banned the sale of alcohol to "Indians" in 1829. Colonial legislation from 1868 on banned the sale and barter of alcohol to Indigenous people and intoxication. In the North-West Territories, distilled alcohol was banned in the early 1870s, and the newly formed Royal North West Mounted Police was created to enforce the law.

CAP. XLII.

An Act providing for the organisation of the Department of the Secretary of State of Canada, and for the management of Indian and Ordnance Lands.

[*Assented to 22nd May*, 1868.]

Preamble.

HER Majesty, by and with the advice and consent of the Senate and House of Commons of Canada, enacts as follows :

Department constituted.

Tenure of office.

1. There shall be a department to be called "The Department of the Secretary of State of Canada," over which the Secretary of State of Canada for the time being, appointed by the Governor General by commission under the Great Seal, shall preside ; and the said Secretary of State shall have the management and direction of the Department, and shall hold office during pleasure.

Under Secretary and officers.

2. The Governor General may also appoint an "Under Secretary of State," and such other officers as may be necessary for the proper conduct of the business of the said Department, all of whom shall hold office during pleasure.

General duties of Secretary.

3. It shall be the duty of the Secretary of State to have charge of the State correspondence, to keep all State records and papers not specially transferred to other Departments, and to perform such other duties as shall from time to time be assigned to him by the Governor General in Council.

To be Registrar General.

4. The Secretary of State shall be the Registrar General of Canada, and shall as such register all Instruments of Summons, Commissions, Letters Patent, Writs, and other Instruments and Documents issued under the Great Seal.

And Superintendent of Indian affairs.

5. The Secretary of State shall be the Superintendent General of Indian affairs, and shall as such have the control and management of the lands and property of the Indians in Canada.

Excerpt from *Indian Act*, 1868.

There is evidence that some Indigenous nations supported alcohol prohibition in the 1800s; however, support was framed within a larger context of loss of land, sovereignty, the extermination of animals, smallpox epidemics and the trade in ammunition and arms by non-Indigenous people to Indigenous people. As mentioned above, the 1876 *Indian Act* consolidated earlier colonial legislation that prohibited alcohol from being sold to and consumed by Status Indians. The introduction of whisky and other hard liquor by heavy drinking white traders had devastating effects for some Indigenous communities. Critics argue that alcohol prohibition did not become a provision of the *Indian Act* solely because of concerns about consumption. Rather, prohibition served as a legal mechanism to further control Indigenous peoples and nations. In addition, although many early white settlers married Indigenous women, by the 1800s, colonial and eugenic fears emerged more strongly in Canada. White settlers viewed the "mixing of the races" as a threat to racial boundaries and ultimately to the white nation. It was believed by temperance advocates that if alcohol were prohibited, there would be less inter-racial mixing between white and Indigenous peoples and less mixed-race children.

Colonialism, and the quest for resources, land and souls, was accompanied by the social and legal discrimination against Indigenous people. The fact that Indigenous nations had their own diverse and long-established political systems, knowledges and cultural and spiritual practices was disregarded. Colonialism positioned Indigenous people as not fully human. White religious and political leaders at that time espoused that the consumption of alcohol was more "injurious to Indians than the whites" because of "their semi-savage condition."[1]

To drink legally, or to vote, those deemed Status Indians had to give up their status. Supplying alcohol to a Status Indian resulted in imprisonment for up to six months and/or a fine of no less than $50 and up to $300. Indian Agents, prosecutors and informers profited from the legislation because half of the fine went to them. Thus they had a vested interest in arresting Status Indians under the *Indian Act* provisions right up until 1936 when this practice was repealed. Also, any Status Indian found to be intoxicated faced imprisonment for up to a month, and if the accused did not provide the name of their supplier, an additional two weeks was added to their sentence. In 1936, the *Indian Act* also added a new provision criminalizing anyone in possession of alcohol or any other intoxicant (such as opiates, cocaine, etc.) in the home of a Status Indian, on or off reserve. Unlike other Canadians, Status Indians were denied a legal space to drink.

Alcohol prohibition for Status Indians lasted right up until 1955 when the *Indian Act* was amended to allow provinces to provide Status Indians the same drinking rights as other Canadians. However, it took many provinces a decade to do so, and some bands chose not to lift the ban on reserves. For more than a century alcohol prohibition created more harm than good. It did not stop Indigenous people from drinking alcohol; instead it encouraged covert and dangerous drinking practices, illegal consumption and selling, and discouraged social drinking.

Thousands of Indigenous people were arrested and imprisoned due to the law. It was a punitive and racialized policy used by Indian Agents and police. It also contributed to enduring stereotypes and legal discrimination against Indigenous people. The *Indian Act* and colonialism in all its many manifestations, including but not limited to alcohol prohibition, the reserve system, residential schools, policing and child apprehension, continues to affect Indigenous families and nations today.

The Scream (permission from artist Kent Monkman, Acrylic on Canvas, 84" x 132", 2017, kentmonkman.com).

OPIUM POPPY

Besides alcohol, settlers brought other plant-based drugs with them. The opium poppy, *Papaver somniferum*, was renowned for centuries and continues today to be an important medicine. Scholars claim that the opium poppy was recognized as an essential medical treatment as far back as the Egyptian, Greek and Roman empires. Opium has long been used for pain management, intestinal ailments, respiratory conditions and infections. It became an important medicine and trade item in India, China, Europe and the Middle East.

The opium poppy is an annual plant that is cultivated for its sap, which is collected and dried to form raw opium. Raw opium is formed into cakes and small balls to be stored and sold on the market. Opium is a narcotic that is consumed in various forms, including smoking and liquid forms.

Opium poppy field (Wellcome Library, London).

Modus extrahendi papaueris succum.

A Mong those powerfull guifts to man infus'd,
What better is thé knowledge of those plants
Which for two thousand yeares were only vs'd

Method of extracting the juice from the poppy, woodcut, Opiologia by Sala (Angelus), 1618 (Wellcome Library, London).

Drug jar for opium made in Britain between 1670 and 1740. The label on the jar stands for "poppy conserve" (Wellcome Images, London, Science Museum).

In the 1700s and 1800s, opiate-based drugs were taken orally, and opiate-based elixirs, teas, patent medicines, cough suppressants and tinctures were consumed in Europe and in Canada. Opiate-based drugs were also unregulated and could be bought in local pharmacies or by mail order. At that time there was no distinction between legal and illegal drugs. Laudanum, an opiate-based tincture, was also consumed during this time. It was often used by white, middle-class women for what were termed as "women's problems."

Papine is the trade name for this popular opium remedy, 1890–1920 (Wellcome Images, London, Science Museum).

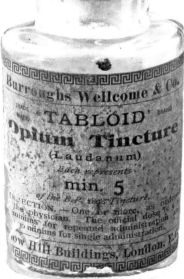

Laudanum, an opium tincture taken orally, was a popular medicine, 1880–1940 (Wellcome Images, London Science Museum,.

Medicine chest for the home or apothecary, containing medicines for a range of illnesses. It includes opiates, emetics, rhubarb, stimulants, such as ginger and lavender, scales and other instruments, 1801–1900 (Wellcome Images, London Science Museum).

Many popular soothing syrups for infants also contained small amounts of opium and alcohol. The syrups were given to infants for teething and to sooth an upset stomach. Historians Virginia Berridge and Griffith Edwards explain that gastro-intestinal problems for infants coupled with poverty and poor housing conditions led to high infant mortality rates in Britain during the 1800s. In the face of these harsh social facts, parents found relief for their infants using soothing syrups.[2] Canadian families faced similar problems.

Mrs. Winslows Soothing Syrup for Children Teething contained opium, 1885 (U.S. National Library of Medicine, A021055).

THE COCA PLANT

The coca plant, *Erythroxylum*, has been grown for thousands of years and is an integral part of cultural and social life in regions of South America. The leaf is chewed and used in teas and other products. The coca leaf is a mild stimulant that contains minerals and nutrients.

Advertisement for Coca-Cola beverage, 1890 (Library of Congress, # 2004671509).

Women gathering leaves of the coca plant at a coca farm in Bolivia, wood carving, 1867 (Wellcome Library, London).

The coca plant was introduced to Western societies after parts of South America were colonized.

However, products made from coca did not become common in Western nations until the late 1800s when it was included in patent medicines, cough drops, wines, and beverages, such as Coca-Cola. Coca-Cola and other drinks made from coca extract were often advertised as temperance beverages.

Coca plant (permission from artist Iain Mitchell-Boyd).

Advertisement for Hall's Coca Wine, 1916 (Wellcome Library, London, Ephemera Collection, by Stephen Smith & Co.).

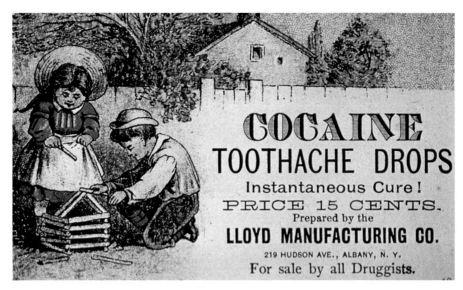

Advertisement for cocaine toothache drops, 1880–1899 (US National Library of Medicine, A021082).

CANNABIS

Cannabis, *Cannabis sativa*, is an ancient plant originally from central Asia, and it is used for medicinal, spiritual and recreational purposes. The cannabis plant contains hundreds of chemical substances and more than one hundred cannabinoids or compounds, tetrahydrocannabinol (THC) being only one of them. The plant also provides fibre, paper, rope, oil and edible seeds. However, outside of its use for these commodities, cannabis products were not used as often for their medicinal properties in Western nations until the mid-nineteenth century. Western imperialism introduced British doctors who travelled and lived in colonial India

Cannabis plant as medicine from "De historia stripivm commentarrii insignes" by Leonhart Fuchs, 1542 (Wellcome Library, London).

and other nations to a wider range of plant drugs. For example, some British doctors who visited India in the 1800s praised cannabis for its euphoric effects and recommended it for medicinal use. It soon became an ingredient in patent medicines and tonics and was recommended for treating migraines, ulcers, painful menstruation and asthma.

Cannabis plant (permission from artist, Iain Mitchell-Boyd).

Although cannabis-based products were never as popular as opiate-based drugs, cannabis products were advertised in the early 1900s for treating mental and physical exhaustion, depression and insomnia. Pharmaceutical companies, such as Squibb and Eli Lilly, produced and sold cannabis products.

In the late 1800s and early 1900s, doctors wrote about the benefits of cannabis, cocaine and opium-based products, and Canadian citizens consumed these medicines. In rural Canada, people relied on plant-based drugs in oral, powder and tablet preparations to care for the health of their family, especially prior to public health care. Doctors were also few and far between and expensive in rural areas.

Plant-based drugs were active ingredients in medicines and tonics available by mail order and at apothecaries and drug stores. Oftentimes ingredients were not fully listed, and producers made wild claims about the healing properties of their patient medicines and tonics.

Plant-based drugs were sold without prescriptions in mail-order catalogues, such as the Simpson Company and Eaton's. Compared to the services of a doctor, these medicines were cheap and available. Many tonics and patent medicines contained only herb mixtures, and some medicines also included alcohol.

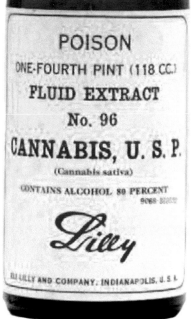

Oral cannabis, marketed by Lilly (permission from David Malmo Levine from his Special Collection).

Bayer's Pharmaceutical Products advertised in the *British Medical Journal* in 1899 (Wellcome Library, London).

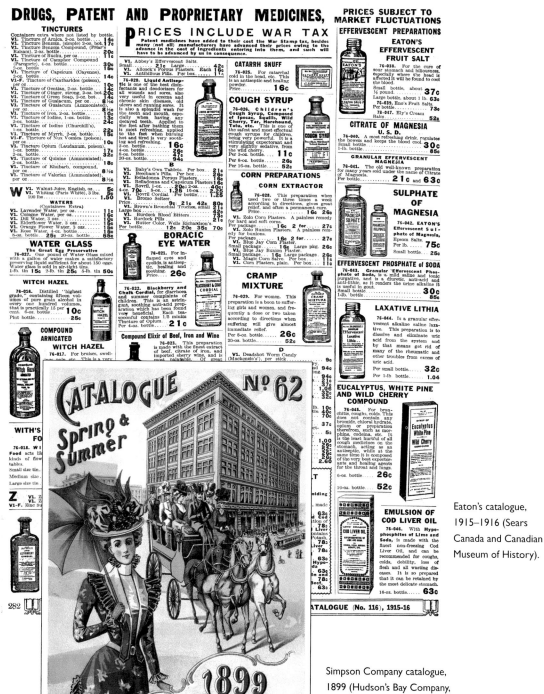

Eaton's catalogue, 1915–1916 (Sears Canada and Canadian Museum of History).

Simpson Company catalogue, 1899 (Hudson's Bay Company, Archives of Manitoba, and Canadian Museum of History).

ISOLATION OF COMPOUNDS FROM PLANTS

In 1803, a German chemist isolated an organic compound (or alkaloid)—morphine—from opium. This is the first time that an active compound was isolated from a plant. Morphine, in its refined state, is more potent than raw opium. It can be taken orally and by injection.

Solution of morphine, first isolated from opium in 1803. The name refers to Morpheius, the ancient Greek god of dreams (Wellcome Images, London, Science Museum).

This date marks the beginning of the pharmaceutical industry's quest for semi-synthetic and synthetic drugs with greater potency and profit. Drugs can be natural (plant-based), refined, semi-synthetic or synthetic. For example, heroin is a semi-synthetic drug that was first derived from the compound morphine in 1898. The coca leaf is a plant that contains many compounds, cocaine being only one of them. The other compounds found in the coca leaf modify cocaine's stimulant effect. In fact, the coca leaf contains vitamins and nutrients. The coca leaf contains about 0.5 percent cocaine; thus products made from powdered coca are similar in potency. In contrast, refined cocaine can be up to 100 percent pure. Equating the coca leaf with refined cocaine, as our contemporary drug laws do, is quite the stretch of imagination.

The coca leaf and industrialized products made with powdered coca leaf, Quito, Ecuador (photographer: Pablo Corral Vega. ID: 77931, National Geographic Creative Photography).

Refined cocaine contains up to 100 percent cocaine (Shutterstock, I.D. 466831727, photo by majo 1122331).

The invention of the syringe in the early 1850s changed drug use. Instead of oral medicines, now drugs like refined morphine and cocaine could be injected, and their effects could be felt more quickly. Prior to the late 1800s and early 1900s, the consumption of opiate, cocaine and cannabis products was a personal matter—there was little stigma attached to using drugs at that time. If a person used a drug regularly they might be seen as a habitual user. The term "addiction," as a concept associated with drug use, was not fully developed then. Even today the term "addiction" is culturally and historically bound, and the concept of addiction is continually changing.

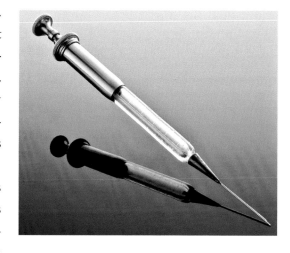

In Canada, opiate use in and of itself was not considered a social problem in the 1700s and 1800s. There were only anecdotal accounts of habitual use. However, attitudes were changing due to Protestant ethics about self-control, sobriety and morality. The increased power of medical professionals, and their growing concerns about unregulated patient medicines, and colonial discourse about outsiders to white, middle-class morality also influenced this change. Drug consumption became more suspect, especially drug use associated with foreigners.

Hypodermic syringe made by Coxeter & Son, 1856–1865, Britain (Wellcome Images, London, Science Museum).

THE OPIUM WARS

Ideas about the use of some forms of plant-based drugs were about to shift dramatically over the 1800s and early 1900s. Several international, national and local events led to changes in the way that raw opium was thought of by citizens of Britain and Canada. Although opium had been imported into China since the eighth century, the smoking of opium began in the late 1500s following the import of tobacco. Smoking opium increased in China in the 1700s and 1800s as the British East India Company brought in chest loads of opium for trading. Although opium was illegal in China, British traders transported the drug from India into the country to trade for tea and other items.

Drying room in an opium factory in India, lithograph by W.S. Sherwill, 1850 (Wellcome Library, London).

The East India Company ship *Nemesis* and other steam ships destroying Chinese junks in Anson's Bay on January 7, 1841, during the Opium Wars (National Maritime Museum, Greenwich, London, 0792, PAH8893).

When China sought to stop the opium trade, two Opium Wars (a term applied by anti-opiate reformers) were fought by England (1839–1842 and 1856–1860) to force the Chinese Government to allow the profitable trade to continue.[3]

The Opium Wars provided British, Canadian and U.S. Christian missionaries at home, and in China and India, to advance their ideas about the evils of opium use, specifically opium smoking, by non-white people in colonized nations. Christian missionaries believed that moderate use of opium (especially in smoking form) was impossible. Protestant missionaries' view on opium in colonized nations was a form of cultural imperialism as they failed to see, especially in India, how opium cultivation and personal use was mainly unproblematic, long standing and relied upon for medicinal purposes. Many supporters of the anti-opiate movement were also members of the temperance movement. Both movements highlighted the physical and moral decline of users and called for prohibition.

Mass meeting under the auspices of the Anti-Opium Urgency Committee, World's Woman's Christian Temperance Union, 1894 (Wellcome Library, London, GC EPH560: 26).

By the end of the 1800s, opium smoking and trafficking became firmly linked to Chinese men, who were depicted as endangering white moral citizens. Britain's imperialist, free trade practices that allowed British merchants to profit from the trade in opium was overlooked or ignored.

In Canada, as the early 1900s began, opium, cocaine and cannabis remained legal and unregulated; however, change was on the horizon. Vancouver, B.C., was soon to become the epicentre of events that led to Canada's first opium law.

NOTES

1. Canada. 1895. *Report of the Royal Commission on the Liquor Traffic Minutes of Evidence.* Ottawa: Canada.
2. Berridge, Virginia, and Griffith Edwards. 1981. *Opium and the People: Opiate Use in Nineteenth Century England.* Toronto: Allan Lane.
3. Lovell, Julia. 2011. *The Opium War: Drugs, Dreams and the Making of China.* Oxford: Picador.

2

The Beginnings of Narcotic Control: 1880s–1920s

For more than a century, the City of Vancouver has played a pivotal role in the formation of drug prohibition and resistance to it. A number of significant events took place in Vancouver that dramatically altered drug policy in Canada. Race continues to be a central feature of Canadian drug policy. After ensuring provisions in the *Indian Act* to prohibit the sale and possession of alcohol to those designated Status Indians by the Federal Government, white Canadians turned their attention to Chinese residents.

Chinese labourers working on the Canadian Pacific Railway in the mountains of B.C., 1884 (Library and Archives Canada, Boorne & May, C-006686B).

Although some Chinese men came to Canada to join the Gold Rush in 1858, a second influx of men arrived in the late 1800s to work on the national railway. The national railway was envisioned by the Federal Government as a project to unite white settlements throughout the Dominion and to provide speedy transport of military units, especially following the Métis Red River resistance in the late 1860s.

At that time Chinese men were seen as honest, hard-working labourers. However, there was also a profit motive involved: Chinese labourers were paid a third of what white labourers received from contractors hired by the Canadian Pacific Railway (CPR) and were given some of the most dangerous jobs.

Chinese workers on a Canadian Pacific Railway ship travelling to Canada to work, date unknown (Vancouver Public Library, 12866).

Camp and work conditions were rough for the Chinese men who worked on the CPR, especially through the mountain terrain of the west coast. When the railway was complete, linking east and west, many Chinese men settled permanently in Vancouver. Although the west coast did not become a British colony until 1849 and part of Canada until 1871, white settlers intended it as a "white Canada," even though the area was home to Indigenous people.

In 1886, the City of Vancouver was founded. The CPR was given prime land by the Federal Government throughout the area. This land was not unoccupied, but was, and is, the traditional homeland of the Coast Salish. However, from Vancouver's inception, city politicians and labour leaders espoused white supremacy. Indigenous people were seen as inferior and outsiders to white "British" Columbia. Many Indigenous people were torn from their traditional lands and, along with Chinese and Japanese people, were denied the vote and discouraged from living in Vancouver. Whereas the *Indian Act* regulated all aspects of Indigenous peoples' lives, the City and Province enacted by-laws to restrict where Chinese and Japanese people could live and work, and even what professions they could work in.

Arrival of first Canadian Pacific Railway passenger train to Vancouver, B.C. 1908 (Vancouver Public Library, 27).

Chinese Canadian family in front of Wah Chong Washing and Ironing, 1895 (City of Vancouver Archives/ AM1376-: CVA 178-2.8).

Following the completion of the national railway in 1885, the Federal Government enacted the first head tax of $50 on all Chinese people immigrating to Canada. No other group of immigrants had to pay a head tax to immigrate to the Dominion. The head tax increased to $500 in 1903, an exorbitant amount of money at that time.

Canadian Illustrated News, April 26, 1879 (Library and Archives Canada/00269 LAC). The cover of the 1879 paper *Canadian Illustrated News,* entitled "The Heathen Chinee in British Columbia," depicts Amor de Cosmos, a Liberal Member of Parliament (and former premier of B.C.), forcing a Chinese immigrant to leave British Columbia. de Cosmos contributed extensively to anti-Asian and anti-Indigenous propaganda.

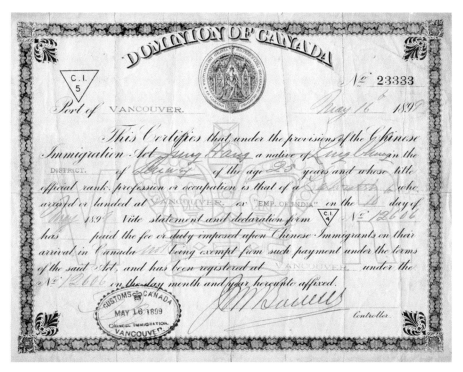

Head Tax Certificate, 1899 (Library and Archives Canada, R1206-178-X-E).

Chinese people were not allowed to own homes or businesses outside of an area designated as Chinatown in the east part of Vancouver. A small concentration of homes and businesses were established there, west of the space delineated as the Japanese quarter. By-laws restricted what professions Chinese people could work in and where they could live and be employed. Despite discrimination and legal barriers, Chinese and Japanese Canadians made Vancouver their home.

Head Tax Certificate, 1913 (Library and Archives Canada, R1206-178-X-E).

Dupont Street in Chinatown, Vancouver, B.C. (now East Pender), 1904 (Vancouver Public Library, 6729).

Although white British Columbians and other Canadians used liquid forms of opium, such as laudanum, elixirs, tonics and patent medicines, they also purchased raw opium. Some Chinese people who used opium consumed it by smoking it. They smoked opium for medicinal purposes, for pain relief and to relax. There are no official statistics; however, given that most Chinese men in the Vancouver area worked long gruelling hours as labourers, servants, and cooks, most likely the majority of those men who smoked opium were not dependant on the drug. [1]

Two wealthy Chinese opium smokers, Gouache painting on rice-paper, nineteenth century (Wellcome Library, London).

From the late 1800s, right up to 1908, thousands of pounds of opium was legally imported to Canada for pharmaceutical companies to prepare patent medicines and other products consumed by white Canadians. Raw opium was also imported to a lesser degree to Chinese opium factories in B.C., which sold it in smoking form. Similar to the head tax imposed on Chinese immigrants, Chinese opium factories had to pay a $500 licensing fee in order to do business in the province; however, pharmaceutical companies making patent medicines containing opium were exempt from the fee. [2]

Fears about smoking opium were also expressed in the media.

Ivory opium pipe (Wellcome Images, London, Science Museum).

An Opium Den: Prevalence of a Deadly Habit Among Chinese in Toronto: A Reporter's Visit to a Den
Globe and Mail, Aug. 20, 1884

It will be remembered that a few weeks ago a statement appeared in these columns with reference to a Chinaman named Ah Chung who had been ruined through the deadly habit of opium smoking.

WOULD SAVE THE SAVAGE,
Prevent the Sale of Opium and Intoxicants
Globe and Mail, Feb 26, 1907

Resolution passed at meeting of Foreign Mission Secretaries in Toronto—
An Address by Rev. Dr. W. F. Crafts on the subject

That a petition should go to the Imperial Parliament urging Great Britain to
join with the United States in presenting a treaty for signature by the other
powers, agreeing to prevent the sale of intoxicants and opium to aboriginal
races [Chinese and other non-white people] was the effect of a resolution
introduced by Rev. Dr. Chown....

On May 30, 1906, the British Parliament, by unanimous vote, declared "the Chinese opium trade morally indefensible" and instructed the Government
"to bring it to a speedy close.

A new surge of racism emerged following an economic slump, leading many white labourers to believe that Chinese and Japanese labourers were taking jobs away from them. In the United States, unfound-
ed fears about Asian "military might" followed the Japanese victory

against the Russian Empire in 1905. White
supremacist propaganda flourished about
the "yellow peril," referring to the belief that
Asian nations hoped to take over the U.S. and
other Western countries. Responding to these
fears, the U.S. Exclusion League was formed
by white labourers and politicians to stop
Asian immigration and competition in the
workplace. In B.C., the Vancouver Trades and
Labour Council supported the Canadian Asi-

Vancouver City Hall,
site of the anti-Asiatic
race riot on September
7, 1907 (Vancouver
Public Library, 19834).

atic Exclusion League in 1907. A parade and demonstration was then
planned to protest Asian immigration and employment in Canada. On
September 7, 1907, a parade of over 8,000 to 9,000 people wound its
way through Vancouver. At the head of the parade, protesters held a
large banner that read "Stand for a White Canada" as they marched to
City Hall (located then at the corner of Main and Hastings). [3]

Boarded up damaged businesses in Chinatown on the corner of Carrall and Pender Streets following the race riot on September 7, 1907 (Vancouver Public Library, 940).

At City Hall a group of white men broke away from the parade, heading east into Chinatown. A riot ensued as they smashed the windows of Chinese-run businesses. The rioters then moved on to the Japanese quarter of the city on Powell Street. However, having been alerted about the violence in the Chinese community, Japanese residents were better prepared, and they eventually succeeded in stopping the rioters. Nevertheless, both communities feared for their physical safety and suffered damage to their property.

The press played a significant role before and following the riot. The media contributed to anti-Asian attitudes by demanding that B.C. remain a white province, portraying Chinese people as inferior outsiders, calling for deportation, and insisting that immigration cease. White settlers in B.C. also showed their support of a white province and nation by wearing "White Canada" ribbons. [4]

Chinese-owned barbershop damaged during the anti-Asiatic race riot on September 7, 1907 (Vancouver Public Library, 941).

Japanese Language School established in 1906, Vancouver, B.C. A few days after the riot, white men attempted to burn the school down (Vancouver Public Library, 85994).

The 1907 race riot made headlines around the world. Within a few days of the anti-Asiatic riot, Japan's consul in Vancouver contacted the prime minister of Canada. In response, Prime Minister Wilfrid Laurier sent the deputy minister of the Department of Labour, William Lyon Mackenzie King, to investigate the damages that the Japanese community suffered during the riot. Following pressure from the Chinese Government, King later investigated damages to Chinese businesses too.

Mackenzie King arrived in Vancouver in September 1907. During his second visit to assess claims, King received a letter on May 29, 1908, from law graduate Peter Hing. Hing was a high profile evangelist moral reformer (his father was a missionary and Presbyterian minister) and also the secretary of the Chinese Anti-Opium League that espoused the idea that "opium is a social evil in this world" that needs to be suppressed. It is not known whether the Chinese Anti-Opium League represented the interests of other Chinese residents in Vancouver's Chinatown. There are no official records of opium smoking at that time. However, as discussed in Chapter 1, Protestant missionaries in and outside of Canada were vocally advocating for an end to the opium trade in China and their campaigns were becoming more mainstream as they gained the ear of prominent politicians in England and Canada. The League requested a meeting with King, who wrote back immediately, agreeing to meet with representatives from the League.

Mackenzie King, deputy minister of the Department of Labour, 1904 (Library and Archives Canada, William James Topley, PA-025990).

In his letter to the League, King outlined his position on opium to them:

> Among the well-wishers of mankind, there can be, I think, but one opinion as to the attitude which should be assumed toward this evil, which, once existent, does so much to destroy not only the lives of individuals, but the manhood of a nation. … I shall certainly deem it a privilege to look into the question while here, and will gladly do my part to obtain the co-operation of the public authorities here and elsewhere in the suppression of this evil. [5]

Shortly afterwards, King met with a deputation of three men from the Chinese Anti-Opium League. A few days later, while speaking to the *Vancouver Daily Province* on June 3, 1908, King declared: "it should be made impossible to manufacture this drug in any part of the Dominion…We will get some good out of this riot yet." [6]

Criminologist Neil Boyd notes that "in the course of three days government policy regarding psychoactive substances effectively changed" in Canada.[7] King travelled back to Ottawa, and a month later he submitted his report, *On the Need for the Suppression of the Opium Traffic in Canada*, to the Federal Government. In the report King argues that opium in smoking form should be criminalized in Canada.

At the same time, a number of other anti-opiate reformers, including Samuel Dwight Chown, a prominent religious leader in Canada and secretary of the Department of Temperance and Moral Reform of the Methodist Church, contacted Sir Wilfrid Laurier and advised him to suppress the importation, manufacture and sale of opium for non-medical use.

To support his view about the danger of opium in smoking form, King included in his report both his communication with the League prior to his earlier meeting in June 1908 and a newspaper article published in the *Vancouver Daily Province* about the "horrible evidence of

MacKenzie King submits his 1908 anti-opium report (Library and Archives Canada, Department of Mines and Technical Surveys, PA-023227).

the dire influence which the opium traffic is exercising among the ranks of British Columbia womanhood." The fear of innocent white women associating with foreign others fuelled opium legislation in Canada. Without a shred of hard evidence to support his claim that smoking

On the Need for the Suppression of the Opium Traffic in Canada
Mackenzie King, July 1, 1908

The Chinese with whom I converse on the subject, assured me that almost as much opium was sold to white people as Chinese, and the habit of opium smoking was making headway, not only among white men and boys, but also among women and girls.... To be indifferent to the growth of such an evil in Canada would be inconsistent with those principles of morality which ought to govern the conduct of a Christian nation.

opium equals harm and degradation, and with no debate on Parliament Hill regarding criminalization, the course of drug policy shifted in Canada and the *Opium Act of 1908* was enacted.

This race-based legislation was aimed at Chinese Canadian men who smoked opium. Following the Act, about seven opium factories were shut down in British Columbia. In the same year that the *Opium Act of 1908* was enacted, the *Proprietary or Patent Medicine Act* was passed. The Act required the labelling of ingredients of patent medicnies, some including heroin, alcohol or cannabis. Penalties for violations of the *Patent Medicine Act*, ranging from $50 to $100 fines, were much lower than

7-8 EDWARD VII.

CHAP. 50.

An Act to prohibit the importation, manufacture and sale of Opium for other than medicinal purposes.

[*Assented to 20th July, 1908.*]

HIS Majesty, by and with the advice and consent of the Senate and House of Commons of Canada, enacts as follows:—

1. Every person is guilty of an indictable offence and liable to imprisonment for three years, or to a penalty not exceeding one thousand dollars and not less than fifty dollars, or to both, who imports for other than medicinal purposes, under regulations to be established by the Minister of Customs, any crude opium or powdered opium, or who manufactures, sells, or offers for sale, or has in his possession for sale, for other than medicinal purposes, any crude opium or powdered opium, or who imports, manufactures, sells, or offers for sale, or has in his possession for sale opium prepared for smoking. *Importation and sale of opium prohibited.*

2. It shall not be an offence under section 1 of this Act to sell or offer for sale, or have in one's possession for sale for other than medicinal purposes, opium in any of the said forms within six months after this Act comes into force, provided such opium is deposited in a customs bonded warehouse for export under regulations to be established by the Minister of Customs. *Sale and possession for limited period permitted.*

OTTAWA: Printed by SAMUEL EDWARD DAWSON, Law Printer to the King's most Excellent Majesty.

Opium Act penalties, which had heavy fines (no less than $50 and up to $1000) and prison penalties (up to three years). It should be pointed out that white Canadians were much more likely to produce and consume patent medicines that might contain opium than to consume opium in smoking form. Patent medicine producers were allowed to continue their trade; in contrast, opium factories were forced to close.

Also in 1908, a private member's bill was introduced to prohibit the importation, manufacure and sale of cigarettes. After heated debate, the bill was defeated; however, two measures were later enacted making it illegal to sell cigarettes to minors under the age of 16 and making it easier for Canadian tobacco producers to compete with foreign producers.[8] The penalty for selling tobacco to a minor was set at $10 for a first offence.

Members of the International Opium Commission, February 26, 1909, Shanghai, China. This meeting was followed by a second in the Hague in 1912 and the signing of the first international drug treaty (Library and Archives Canada, PA-117255).

After initiating drug prohibition at home, Mackenzie King began his rounds outside of Canada, paving the way for an international drug control system. King set himself up as a leader in prohibitionist drug control.

NATIONS UNITED IN GOOD CAUSE:
The Conference for the Abolition of the Opium Traffic
Globe and Mail, May 8, 1909

CHINESE ARE SINCERE
Canada's Representative Tells of the Gathering

How Canada has pointed the way in regard to reform leading to the abolition of the opium traffic was an interesting feature of an interview which *The Globe* obtained from Mr. W. L. Mackenzie King, M.P., C.M.G., the representative of the Dominion at the great international conference held in Shanghai during the early part of the year.

"It was particularly interesting, so far as Canada was concerned, to notice that the Dominion had already adopted legislation along the lines advocated, both in regard to the suppression of the use of opium and of morphine in patent medicines and other forms. It was also an interesting fact that the American delegation generously admitted that their legislation for the suppression of the traffic in the United States had been copied from Canada."

Meanwhile in Montreal, the Children's Aid Society began to wage an anti-cocaine campaign supported by political allies, religious leaders, police chiefs, Montreal Women's Club and other civil organizations.

Cocaine

The cocaine habit must be stamped out of Canada.
It is undermining our boyhood and cutting away the moral fibre of our girls.
It is turning our young people into criminals and imbeciles....

The first samples are distributed to children, free.
The samples create a demand and the children come again.
It is refused unless they bind themselves to absolute secrecy.
A few doses and the habit has grown.
THE CHILDREN MUST HAVE THEIR 'DOPE'
All moral sense is lost and in a few months our girls and boys are ruined.

Montréal Children's Aid Society Flyer, 1910-1911 [9]

Newspaper articles in Quebec depicted crazed cocaine demons and criminal enterprises trafficking the substance. These news articles and other sources were citied by Mackenzie King as he sought support in the House of Commons to strengthen the *Opium Act of 1908.*

CHILDREN USE COCAINE
The Globe, April 8, 1910

THE WOMAN IS A COCAINE FIEND AND NOT LIKELY TO RECOVER
The Globe, October 20, 1910

CRAZED WITH COCAINE:
Woman runs barefoot in Montreal Streets
The Globe, November 29, 1910

THE COCAINE HABIT
The Globe, November 25, 1911

TO STAMP OUT THE DRUG HABIT
Globe and Mail, Feb. 2, 1911

Drastic Legalisation Approved by the Commons

COCAINE THE GREAT FOE

Startling Statistics as to Its Widespread Use.

The Minister of Labor Places Before Parliament Facts That Lead to Prompt Action—Druggists Approve of the Proposal.

Ottawa
This is the bill of the Hon. W.L. Mackenzie King, Minister of Labor, to forbid under severe penalties the importation, manufacture, sale or use of opium, morphine and cocaine for other than scientific or medicinal purposes.

At home, after much debate, the *Opium and Drug Act of 1911* was passed. Other drugs were added to the schedule. The Act criminalized cocaine and morphine for non-medical or non-scientific use. Foremost, the Act criminalized possession of these drugs, opium prepared for smoking and people found in opium dens. Police powers were expanded, and a search warrant was now easily obtained if there was reasonable cause to suspect that drugs were concealed for purposes outside of medical or scientific use. The burden of proof fell on the accused to prove innocence, a marked departure from long established criminal law principles. Following the 1908 and 1911 Acts, law enforcement more vigorously profiled Chinese residents and opium dens from 1912 onwards.

In 1908, Canada chose to take two different drug control routes. One for tobacco and alcohol, allowing the legal sale and production of them. Early on, commerical interests, government control, and consumer demand shaped to-

Vancouver Police Department patrol wagon outside No. 1 Fire Station, 1914 (Vancouver Public Library, 985).

bacco and alcohol control. More recently, public health and education accompany alcohol and tobacco regulation in Canada. The other route for specific drugs like opium was that of criminalizing the importation, production and sale for non-medical purposes. In 1911, the simple possession of opium, morphine and cocaine was criminalized. The second policy route would create disastrous long-term consequences.

1912 - Narcotic Convictions: 342

1915 - Narcotic Convictions: 1,375[10]

WORLD WAR I

The war years from 1914 to 1918, under the federal leadership of Conservative Prime Minister Robert Borden, did not divert Ottawa's attention away from drug prohibition. In fact, federal restrictions on alcohol came into place from March 1918 until the end of 1919. Although there was a slight drop in narcotic convictions in 1917, convictions steadily increased from 1918 onward. At that time, illegal drugs were depicted as a threat to the war effort and the morality of the nation. Illegal drug use was also associated with foreign others, outsiders to the Dominion. The Russian Revolution in 1917 and political upheavals throughout Eu-

Kingston Penitentiary, 1919 (Archives of Ontario, C 285-1-0-0-331).

rope rocked Western capitalist democratic nations, which felt threatened by the "Red Scare." The Winnipeg General Strike in 1919, which, spurred on by high unemployment and inflation, was violently suppressed by law enforcement, including the arrest and deportation of labour leaders and participants. Law enforcement was active arresting "enemy aliens" they deemed a threat to the nation, especially Chinese Canadians.

The first decade of narcotic control came to an end. White Canadians paid little attention to its first narcotic laws assuming the acts were passed to regulate only "devious" Chinese opium smokers, but it soon became apparent that a moral panic about drugs and the people associated with them was gearing up. The net of prohibitionist control would expand to encompass many more people. Deportation (of Chinese men) and prison time would become more commonplace for poor and low-status people convicted of a drug offence. By 1922, over 60 percent of all drug convictions were for Chinese residents. As the 1920s progressed, Canada's drug laws became harsher.

NOTES

1. Carstairs, Catherine. 2006. *Jailed for Possession. Illegal Drug Use, Regulation, and Power in Canada*, 1920-1961. Toronto: University of Toronto Press.
2. Boyd, Neil. 1984. "The origins of Canadian narcotics legislation: The process of criminalization in historical context." *Dalhousie Law Journal*, 8(1).
3. Price, John. 2007. "Orienting the Empire: Mackenzie King and the aftermath of the 1907 race riots." *BC Studies*, 156.
4. Ward, Peter. 2008. *White Canada Forever*. Montreal: McGill-Queen's University Press.
5. Canada. 1908. Report by W.L. Mackenzie King, *On the Need for the Suppression of the Opium Traffic in Canada*, no. 36b.
6. *The Vancouver Daily Province*, June 3, 1908.
7. Boyd, 1984.
8. Green, Melvyn. 1986. "A history of Canadian narcotics control: The formative years." In N. Boyd (Ed.), *The Social Dimensions of Law*.
9. Giffen, P.J., Shirley Endicott, and Sylvia Lambert. 1991. *Panic and Indifference: The Politics of Canada's Drug Laws*. Ottawa: Canadian Centre on Substance Abuse.
10. All drug offences in *Busted* are drawn from: Keighley, Kathryn. 2017. "Police-reported crime statistics in Canada, 2017." *Juristat*. Ottawa: Canadian Centre for Justice Statistics; Cotter, Adam, Jacob Greenland, and Maisie Karam. 2015. "Drug-related offences in Canada, 2013." *Juristat*. Ottawa: Canadian Centre for Justice Statistics; Desjardins, Norm and Tina Hotton. 2004. "Trends in drug offences and the role of alcohol and drugs in crime." *Juristat*. 24(1); Dauvergne, Mia. 2009. "Trends in police-reported drug offences in Canada." *Juristat*. 29(2). Ottawa: Canadian Centre for Justice Statistics; Giffen, P.J., Shirley Endicott, and Sylvia Lambert. 1991. *Panic and Indifference: The Politics of Canada's Drug Laws*. Ottawa: Canadian Centre on Substance Abuse.

3

Reefer Madness:
1920s-1930s

The 1920s began with further international agreements to control the drug trade. Canada was now a member of the Opium Advisory Committee of the League of Nations.

The decade also began with a strengthening of Canada's drug laws and the passing of the *Opium and Narcotic Drug Act* of 1920. The newly formed federal Department of Health maintained control of the *Opium and Narcotic Drug Act*. Following the election of William Lyon Mackenzie King to prime minister in 1921, the Opium and Narcotic Drug Branch, renamed the Narcotic Division shortly afterwards, was also established. Formed from the Royal Northwest Mounted Police and the Dominion Police, the new Royal Canadian Mounted Police

League of Nations, Geneva, Opening Session, 1920 (United Nations Photo Library).

(RCMP) would take on the primary role of enforcing the new drug laws throughout the Dominion, alongside local police. Unlike the preceding decade, these changes centralized institutional power, legal authority and law enforcement through the Narcotic Division to expand prohibition in Canada. Thus, the "father of drug prohibition," Mackenzie King, took the lead once again in forming prohibitionist policy.

Following this expanded drug prohibition in Canada, there really were no government-funded drug treatment provisions (only private treatment in sanitariums) for individuals who used or were dependent on newly criminalized drugs such as morphine and heroin, nor were drug substitution treatments available for people addicted to narcotics in Canada as they were in Britain and the United States. At that time, if medically advisable, British doctors retained the right to prescribe narcotics to people who were dependent on opioids. In the U.S., about forty publically funded (city and state) clinics initially provided narcotic treatment, including heroin or morphine maintenance following the enactment of American federal drug law, the *Harrison Act* in 1914. Later in the U.S., two federally funded "narcotic farms" provided drug treatment, the first of which opened in 1935 in Lexington, Kentucky.

In Canada, the Narcotic Division (renamed the Division of Narcotic Control in 1948) maintained primary control of drug and addiction policy and was vehemently opposed to drug maintenance programs. Instead, the Division advocated for abstinence and prison for those individuals who could not comply. Canadian doctors were not allowed to prescribe drugs for maintenance purposes to people identified as "addicts." By 1925, the maximum penalty for issuing a prescription for non-medical use was five years, and the law was further strengthened

RCMP on Cambie St., Vancouver, 1936 (Vancouver Public Library, 19354).

Left to right: Nellie McClung, Alice Jamieson and Emily Murphy were moral reformers who campaigned for the vote for women, temperance and drug control, 1918 (City of Edmonton Archives).

The first of a series of articles by Emily Murphy published in *Maclean's* about the drug menace in Canada, February 15, 1920 (Archives, University of Toronto).

in 1929: doctors could also be charged with a criminal offence for not providing information that the Narcotic Branch requested. Some doctors were arrested and convicted under these new laws.

On the home front, a new moral reformer was also about to enter the scene.

Emily Murphy was a magistrate and strident moral reformer in Canada. She campaigned not only for the vote for women but also for temperance and drug prohibition. In the early 1920s she wrote a series of articles in *Maclean's Magazine* about the new drug menace, drug trafficking and racialized Others threatening the white nation.

The articles were published as a book in 1922 titled *The Black Candle*. Among other concerns, Murphy warned about the dangers of smoking opium and the deprivation users would suffer. She writes that every "drug fiend is a liar." In her article, Murphy links opium smoking to a host of problems, includ-

"When she acquires the habit, she does not know what lies before her; later she does not care."—Chapter I, Part I.

"An open-eyed insensate in the dread Valley of the Shadow of the Drug."—Chapter I, Part I.

Photos and excerpts from *The Black Candle*, by Emily Murphy, 1922.

ing crime, and women's sexual immorality, "consorting with the lowest classes of yellow and black men," illegitimate and "half-blood infants" and the abandonment of family and home.[1] Murphy argues that white women in close proximity to racialized men would lead to their inevitable downfall and would threaten the white Christian nation.

Emily Murphy had much to say about corrupt Chinese men, opium smoking, drug dens, trafficking and the corruption of Christian moral nations, she was equally disturbed by marijuana consumption: "Marijuana addicts become raving maniacs and are liable to kill or indulge in any form of violence to other persons."[2]

Emily Murphy's writing about the menace of drugs was accompanied at that time by citizen- and newspaper-led anti-drug campaigns in a number of cities, such as Montreal, Toronto, and Vancouver. These campaigns by local Rotary Clubs, Kiwanis Clubs, Gyros Clubs, Child Welfare Associations and Police Chiefs, were aided by media campaigns that sought to educate Canadians about the "Chinese menace" and to offer solutions: the abolition of Chinatowns in Canada, the deportation of Chinese people and harsher drug laws.

Book cover of *The Writing on the Wall*, 1921.

In 1921, the *Vancouver Sun* published a novel, *The Writing on the Wall*, by Glynn-Ward. The novel captured the anti-Asian prejudice of white British Columbians at that time. The novel is set in Vancouver and features "foul" opium dens, "soul-killing fumes of opium" and a wealthy white couple threatened by corrupt Chinese men.

The anti-drug campaigns in the early 1920s were integral to the anti-Asian campaigns to exclude Chinese people from entering, living and working in Canada. These campaigns resulted in the enactment of the *Chinese Exclusion Act* of 1923, which, with few exceptions, banned Chinese people from entering Canada, created harsher drug laws and intensified police focus on Chinese people. The deportation of Chinese men convicted of a drug offence was already included in the *Opium and*

Narcotic Drug Act in 1922.

Due to fears about some drugs and racial hostility and discrimination towards Chinese men, the *Opium and Narcotic Drug Act* was strengthened in 1922, and in 1923 marijuana was added to the drug schedule with no debate in Parliament or evidence that it was a dangerous drug. By 1925, vehicles could be confiscated if drugs were found in them, and in 1929 whipping was added to the penalties for drug offences. Fines became mandatory in addition to higher minimum penalties and hard labour. Significantly, imprisonment became mandatory for most drug offences.

1922
Number drug convictions: **1,858**
Percentage of convicted individuals of Chinese ethnicity: **60** percent

1924
Deported from Canada after being convicted of a drug offence: **154**
Number of deported individuals of Chinese ethnicity: **125**

"Police, Customs Officers, pose with drugs recovered after one of the pick-up boats was intercepted. The vests worn by the officers were used by smugglers to transport opium. Customs Preventive Service was Canada's version of Border Patrol. At its height, the Preventive Service had vehicles, horseback teams, aircraft and even a gunboat on the St. Lawrence," 1920s (Vancouver Police Museum, P03717).

Vancouver High School Students at Unemployed March, 1935 (Vancouver Public Library, 8808).

THE DEPRESSION

During the 1930s, the Canadian Narcotic Division continued to consolidate its power and argued that drugs and the people who used them were a threat to the nation, even though few people used criminalized drugs at that time. However, around the world, nations grappled with an economic crisis beginning in 1929 that was characterized by huge levels of unemployment: the Great Depression. For a decade, governments struggled with how to deal with the crisis. Similar to the Red Scare following World War I, governments eyed labour organizers, workers, communists and socialists as threats. However, families, students, teachers and whole communities supported the unemployed workers. As the Depression wore on, students, workers and families took to the streets in Canada to protest against joblessness, the failure of capitalism and the Government's weak response to their plight. They organized to pressure the Federal Government, and Conservative Prime Minister R. B. Bennett, to offer support to workers and families.

Mother's Day March in Vancouver, organized by the Mother's Council to support the unemployed, May 12, 1935 (Pacific Tribune Collection).

In Vancouver the plan to undertake the "On-to-Ottawa Trek" was created. In early June 1935, approximately a thousand unemployed men boarded CPR freight trains to Ottawa to petition the Federal Government about the plight of unemployed workers and their families, the infringement of their civil liberties and the dismal conditions of government work camps, which were set up and run by the Department of Defence in some rural areas of the country. The Trek grew as more and more workers joined together and local communities came out to feed and shelter them on their journey. The Trek ended in Regina because the CPR, supported by an order from the Prime Minister, refused to allow the unemployed workers to travel farther. A small delegation of men went on to Ottawa while the rest of the workers waited in the Regina Exhibition Grounds. The talks in Ottawa failed, and the delegation returned to Regina to peacefully disband. Prime Minister Bennett then ordered the Trek leaders to be arrested, and on July 1, 1935, the RCMP and local constables stormed a public meeting of the unemployed workers. Dozens of people were injured, and 130 workers were arrested.

During the Depression, a number of anti-marijuana morality films were produced deflecting attention away from the failed economy and the plight of unemployed workers. Although these were U.S. productions, they were shown in Canada. The first two films, *Assassin of Youth* (1935) and M*arihuana: The Weed with Roots in Hell* (1936), played at the Plaza in Vancouver in the mid-1930s. Some believe that the films, along with *Reefer Madness* (1936), were made with the approval of Harry Anslinger, the Commissioner of the U.S. Federal Bureau of Narcotics. In 1937, Anslinger published an article in *The American Magazine* titled, "Marijuana Assassin of Youth." The article claims that under the influence of marijuana, youth go on crime sprees, commit "sex attacks," murder and become insane.[3] At that time, Anslinger was intent on criminalizing marijuana in the U.S. He employed lurid fictional tales to support prohibition. He also praised Canada for leading the way in criminalizing the plant in 1923. The films, similar to Anslinger's article, depicted white middle-class teenagers as vulnerable to marijuana and the evil dealers who introduced the drug to them. Once the teens in the films smoke marijuana, they are depicted as becoming immediately addicted, going insane and becoming criminals, and in some cases murderers. Young women in the films are depicted as losing any

Unemployed Trek workers attacked by RCMP and local constables on July 1, 1935, in Regina, Saskatchewan (R-B171-3, Provincial Archives of Saskatchewan).

Marijuana Considered Most Vicious Narcotic
The Globe and Mail, Feb. 9, 1938

Marijuana, a harmless-looking weed that grows in profusion in some Southwest States and is common in Canada, is considered by the U.S. Federal Bureau of Investigation to be ten times more powerful than cocaine and the source of the most menacing narcotic problem facing the American Continent.

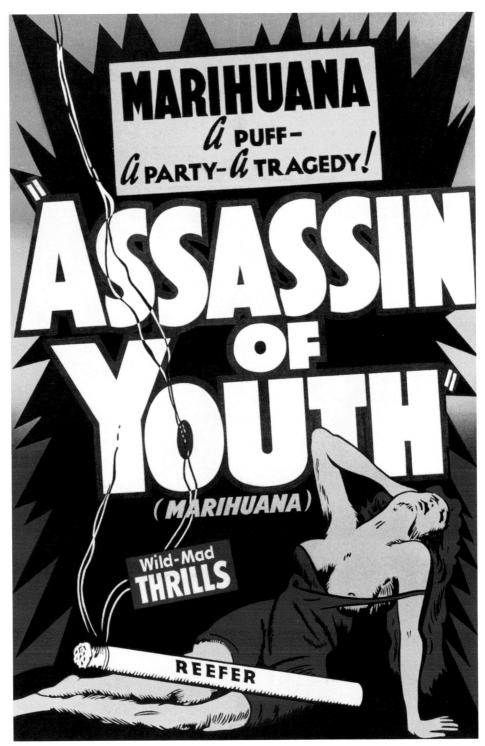

Poster for the film *Assassin of Youth*, 1935 (Photofest).

Toronto Daily Star, Feb. 22, 1938

Marijuana Smokers Seized with Sudden Craze to Kill: Officer Warns Insidious Weed is Even Supplied to School Children.

sense of morality and their degradation follows quickly. By 1937, the federal *Marijuana Tax Act* was enacted in the U.S. However, in Canada and the U.S., few people used marijuana. In Canada, following the criminalization of marijuana in 1923, there were no convictions until 1937, resulting in four possession convictions. Between the years 1937 to 1940 there were twenty-three convictions.[4] The number of marijuana possession arrests remained under twenty-five a year right up until the early 1960s, but even then, it was not until 1967 that marijuana possession arrests began to rise rapidly.[5] Nevertheless law enforcement and moral reformers like

Emily Murphy warned that there was an epidemic of marijuana fiends.

Supported by Prime Minister Mackenzie King (who was elected again in 1935), Colonel Sharman, Chief of the Division of Narcotic Control in Canada, and Harry Anslinger of the Federal Bureau of Narcotics in the U.S. met to better coordinate their efforts to control marijuana in March 1938.

Left to right, Canadian Chief of Narcotic Division, Colonel C.H.L. Sharman, meets with Harry Anslinger, the Director of the U.S. Federal Bureau of Narcotics, and Stephen Gibbons on March 24, 1938, to plan closer cooperation in marijuana regulation between the two countries (U.S. Library of Congress).

Marihuana (*The Weed with Roots in Hell*) and *Assassin of Youth*, played in Vancouver, B.C. in the 1930s (Vancouver Public Library, 11050).

ADDICT FILES

Starting in the late 1920s, the Narcotic Division expanded their surveillance of pharmacies, pharmacists, criminal addicts, traffickers and professional addicts (doctors, nurses and pharmacists) known to them. They stepped up their surveillance by keeping comprehensive files, from 1928 to the early 1970s, on people they labelled as "addicts," "traffickers" and "doctors" in order to better regulate their activities and to convict them. Consequently, the small, and visible group of people who used criminalized drugs experienced long prison sentences, whipping and deportation. This was especially true for those who were poor or from the working class.[6]

Colonel Sharman, the Chief of the Narcotic Division from 1927 to 1946, was an active contributor to the comprehensive addict files in Ottawa. The files contained prosecutors' notes and news clippings of drug arrests and convictions and letters from and to pharmacists, doctors and law enforcement agents pertaining to each "known" addict. Some files held information about the suspect for more than thirty years. In one case, George Johnston was arrested in 1937 for possessing three capsules of morphine. One of the capsules only had trace amounts of the drug. Johnston was convicted and sentenced to prison for six months and fined $200.

> COPY FOR FILE
> No. S-15590
> ORIGINAL ON FILE
> NO. 5-2442
> LMacG/IMP
>
> Ottawa, March 7, 1938
>
> Dear Sir,
>
> Would you be good enough to forward to this Department for disposal under the provisions of the Opium and Narcotic Drug Act, the narcotic exhibits seized in connection with the case of George Johnston, who was sentenced on November 26th, 1937 to six months' imprisonment, fined $200.00 or in default of payment to an additional six months in gaol.
>
> Yours faithfully,
>
> C.H.L. Sharman,
> Chief, Narcotic Division
>
> A.J. Christie, Esq.,
> Deputy Prothonotary,
> Law Courts Building,
> Winnipeg, Man.

Letter from Colonel Sharman requesting information about narcotics seized in an arrest in 1937. *Narcotics, Geo. Johnston, Winnipeg, Man.*© Government of Canada (Reproduced with the permission of Library and Archives Canada (2015). Library and Archives Canada/Department of Health fonds.../RG 29 Volume 3331 File 327-J-24).

If he was unable to pay the fine, which would have been likely during the end of the Depression, an additional six months could have been added to his prison sentence.

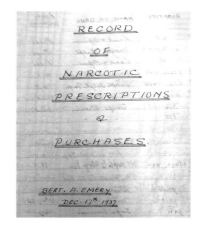

Record of Narcotic Prescriptions and Purchases, 1937 (City of Vancouver Archives, Narcotics Register, Bertram Emery fonds, AM303-S2).

Pharmacists were required to record every prescription and purchase of newly criminalized drugs. By 1920, pharmacists could be charged with a criminal offence if they failed to comply, and they could be charged for dispensing drugs to people who did not have a prescription. A number of criminalized drugs, such as heroin, opium and cocaine, were still available by prescription to treat medical conditions; however, doctors could not prescribe them to treat addiction, and the Narcotic Division scrutinized records looking for offenders.

DATE	QUANTITY	NAME OF DRUG	FORM DISPENSED	Rx NO.
1937 Dec. 29th	v̄iii	Lead + Opium	Pills	A 1 N
" 29-	2 - ½ gr. T.T.	Morph. Sulph.	Caps.	A 2 N
" 31	v̄i	Lead + Opium	Pills	A 3 N
1938 Jan. 8th	1 tube x̄x̄v̄	Morph. Sulph. ½ gr.	H.T.	A 4 N.
" 23rd	1 " x̄x̄v	Morph. Sulph. ¼ gr.	H.T.	A 5 N.
Feb. 14th	4 ozs.	Terpo Dionin	Mist.	A 6 N.
" 28	ʒ̄iv	Terpo Dionin	Mist.	A 7 N.
Mar. 7th	ʒ̄iv	"	"	A 8 N
" 19th	ʒ̄iv	" "	"	A 9 N
" 30	ʒ̄iss	Elix. Terpin Hyd + Heroin	Mist.	A 10 N
April 18	v̄i	H.T. morph. ¼ gr.	H.T.	A 11 N
May 17	1 tube xxv	HT Morph ¼ Atrop 1/150	1 + T	A 12 N

Record of Narcotic Prescriptions and Purchases, 1937 (City of Vancouver Archives, Narcotics Register, Bertram Emery fonds, AM303-S2).

As the 1930s wore on the Narcotic Division, under the leadership of Colonel Sharman, continued to consolidate its power and legal apparatus to control a small population of people. Unlike people who used legal drugs such as alcohol or tobacco, people who used illegal drugs were constructed by the Division as criminals lacking morality. By 1938, the drug schedule contained eleven different groups of criminalized drugs and their derivatives, including opium, cocaine (including the coca leaf), cannabis, Eucaine, morphine, heroin, codeine and other narcotics such as codeine. During the following decade, Ottawa would prove to be even more committed to prohibitionist policies, even during the war years that were about to unfold as Canada entered World War II.

NOTES

1. Murphy, Emily. 1920. "The grave drug menace." *Maclean's Magazine*.
2. Murphy, Emily. 1922/1973. *The Black Candle*. Toronto: Thomas Allen
3. Anslinger, Harry J., with Courtney Ryley Cooper. July 1937. "Marijuana assassin of youth." *The American Magazine*, 121(1).
4. Josie, Gordon. 1947. *A Report on Drug Addiction in Canada*. Ottawa: Department of National Health and Welfare.
5. Giffen, P.J., Shirley Endicott, and Sylvia Lambert. 1991. *Panic and Indifference: The Politics of Canada's Drug Laws*. Ottawa: Canadian Centre on Substance Abuse.
6. See Carstairs, Catherine. 2006. *Jailed for Possession. Illegal Drug Use, Regulation, and Power in Canada*, 1920-1961. Toronto: University of Toronto Press.

4

The Criminal Addict and Psychedelics: 1940s-1950s

Although Ottawa kept its attention on drug prohibition during the war years, the government's attention fell more fully on the "drug problem" following World War II. The new international Protocol on Control of Narcotic Drugs, which also included synthetic drugs, was signed in Paris in 1948. On the domestic front, concern about "criminal addicts" geared up.

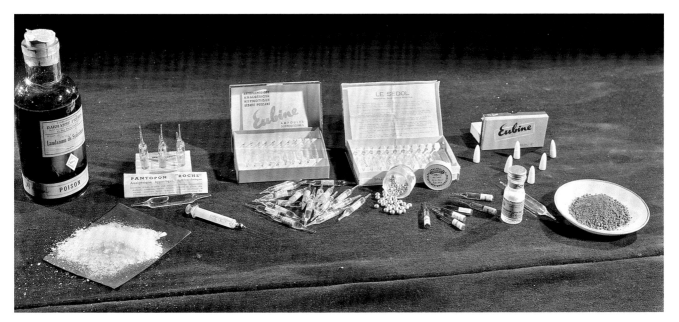

Natural drugs already included in international conventions included: laudanum, cocaine, morphine, opium, and belladonna. The new Protocol on Control of Narcotic Drugs included synthetic drugs and was signed in Paris in November 1948 (United Nations).

1945 Drug Law Enforcement
Drug convictions: **212**
Drug possession convictions: **189** (**89** percent)
Marijuana convictions: **0**

The label "criminal addicts" was a term applied by the Division of Narcotics and the RCMP as early as the 1920s, and the term was later adopted by other professionals in Canada. Criminal addicts, a relatively small population, were subject to an incredible amount of police surveillance and prison time in Canada. From the 1940s on, though, the term was used more frequently. The label of criminal addict was applied to people who were addicted to illegal drugs but not to those addicted to alcohol. Alcoholism was perceived as an illness and a public health problem. Narcotic addiction was seen as a criminal matter. The concept of the criminal addict implied that criminal behaviour preceded addiction. Therefore, it was purported that even if abstinence were achieved, these individuals would still be criminals and a risk to society. It was believed that there was no cure for the criminal addict; thus treatment, including drug substitution treatment, was unnecessary, with abstinence being the preferred goal.

Between 1930 and 1946, 75 percent of all drug convictions were for possession and 73 percent of all drug convictions in Canada resulted in prison time. Although both New Brunswick (21) and Manitoba (289) had few drug convictions in that time period, a higher proportion of people in these provinces were sentenced to penitentiaries (for sentences above two years) than other provinces. Women made up a minority of the total convictions (ranging from 5 to 7 percent) with an increase in convictions between 1941 and 1946. About 18 percent of all drug convictions in this period were for men born in China, which was a significant decrease from convictions in the 1920s.[1]

Before World War II, illegal drug users used a wide range of narcotics, such as opium, morphine, codeine and heroin. Between 1930 and 1946, opium (781 convictions) remained the most common drug involving possession convictions, followed by morphine (627 convictions) and heroin possession (527). Cocaine (65) and cannabis (25) possession convictions were rare.[2] Restrictions on codeine during the war and the unavailability of other drugs led to changes in drug use.

Following World War II and the closure of the opium dens and the deportation of Chinese residents arrested for drug offences, drug use in Canada slowly shifted from smoking opium to the injection and consumption of heroin and morphine. Canadian law enforcement was class biased. Police began profiling a relatively small group of visible "criminal addicts," the poor and working class comprised of white heroin users in Montreal, Toronto and Vancouver. These heroin users also included some young people.

After World War II, psychiatrists also became active in the treatment of addiction, especially to heroin. New knowledge advanced by psychiatrists at that time claimed that addiction to criminalized drugs was a psychiatric disorder as well as a criminal activity. Psychiatrists in Canada worked hand in hand with the Division of Narcotic Control, and poor and working-class people who were addicted to heroin and other criminalized drugs were now labelled as pathological as well as criminal. People falling outside of heteronormative norms were seen as even more deviant. Secure prison units were advanced as the most appropriate site for limited treatment efforts.

In 1946, RCMP Constable H. F. Price published an article titled "The Criminal Addict." He conducted fifty-two interviews with arrested drug offenders. He explains that the white women he interviewed were all "prostitutes" and engaged in promiscuous sexual relations. He describes a young 21-year-old woman as a "sullen foul-tongued girl, mentally dull and utterly lacking in any moral sense."[3] He also claims that the Chinese men he interviewed were of the "coolie class." Ideas put forth by Constable Price about women, racialized men and class are similar to those espoused in the 1920s and 1930s.

Constable Price writes that the most "popular theory" put forth by his arrested interviewees is that government-operated clinics should be established so that they could receive narcotics legally and not have to resort to crime to support their drug use. Constable Price also recommended education to contain the association of criminal addicts with moral citizens through lectures, newspaper articles and films. The National Film Board of Canada complied.

In 1948, the Canadian National Film Board (NFB) produced its first

Drug Addict, 1948 (National Film Board).

documentary about illegal drugs, trafficking and addiction, titled *Drug Addict* and directed by Robert Anderson. With the RCMP, the film was produced for the Division of Narcotic Control and the Department of National Health and Welfare. In the film, viewers are introduced to criminal addicts, law enforcement, criminal regulation and new psychiatric perspectives. This 34-minute, black-and-white, "realist" voice-over documentary was created as an educational tool for law agents and medical professionals in Canada. *Drug Addict* was praised in Canada and won a Canadian Film Awards in 1949 for best documentary.

The film is set in Montreal and graphically depicts the traffic of drugs from foreign countries into Canada. Although the narrator claims that all races are involved, the storyline and visuals make clear that the opium poppy is grown, harvested and smuggled into Canada by racialized Others. The illegal drug trade is described by the narrator as a "stain on the body politic," who also claims that a "pound of opium can be bought in Bombay" is worth "$15,000" once it reaches Canada.

Reinforcing ideas about criminality and out of control behaviour, the narrator also asserts that "addicts" must have their drug "several times a day… [they have] no choice" and that they are involved in a life of crime, often ending up in prison for most of their life.

Near the end of *Drug Addict*, the narrator introduces psychiatry as a

Extraction of sap from the poppy pod, *Drug Addict*, 1948 (National Film Board).

Canadian opium traffickers, *Drug Addict*, 1948 (National Film Board).

profession that can work with criminal justice to provide treatment for some young white men—those new to the world of heroin—in secure, psychiatric units in prisons. The narrator argues that young "addicts" would be separate from long-term criminal addicts in the general prison population. Although sympathetic to young white men newly introduced to heroin, the film's narrator strongly opposes all forms of drug maintenance treatment for people addicted to narcotics and reasserts the claim that "[drug maintenance] clinics spread addiction." The narrator declares that the "solution to addiction to drugs is curing the addict." At the very end of the film, the key role of drug prohibition is reinforced in a scene where law enforcement agents conduct a drug raid. The narrator concludes: "Law enforcement and control always [have a] dominant role in drug regulation."

In the year that *Drug Addict* was produced, 1948, there were only 316 drug convictions in Canada. Although drug arrests do not tell us how many people in Canada used illegal drugs or experienced problematic use, it was not widespread at this time. However, a small group of illegal drug users

A young man's descent into heroin addiction and immorality, *Drug Addict*, 1948 (National Film Board).

were well known to law enforcement. As noted above, these were poor and working-class white people, mostly, and were opium, heroin and morphine users living in Montreal, Toronto and Vancouver.

In 1948, women who used illegal heroin or cocaine were perceived by law enforcement, and medical and social work professionals, as more deviant than men. They were seen as sexually immoral and, having abandoned gender norms, incapable of being good wives or moth-

Local Canadian drug dealer preparing drugs to sell on the illegal market, *Drug Addict*, 1948 (National Film Board).

ers. Poor and working-class women who used criminalized drugs were also depicted as both promiscuous and sex workers, even when research findings proved otherwise.

The Canadian National Film Board produced their second documentary on heroin addiction in 1956. The film, *Monkey on the Back*, reiterates similar claims made in *Drug Addict* about the nature of addiction, the criminal addict, the consequences of heroin addiction and the primacy of law enforcement. The film is sympathetic to the main character, Dick Smith, a white man addicted to heroin in an unnamed city in Canada. Despite being fictional, the narrator, a police officer, tells the audience that

Prison time is inevitable for those using criminalized drugs, *Drug Addict*, 1948 (National Film Board).

Dick could be any "addict" in any Canadian city. The narrator states that Dick was just released from prison and "will be dead by midnight." The audience is told that Dick Smith has been involved in fourteen years of petty crime including shoplifting, theft, possession of narcotics and break and entry. He has served eight prison terms. The narrator claims that Dick is "known to the police as a criminal addict.... he is a man with a weakness, a monkey on his back." At the beginning of the film the viewer is introduced to Dick's loving wife and children, but his family soon abandons him because of his heroin use. In prison once again, Dick suffers from the agony of withdrawal—no medical treatment is offered. The withdrawal scene is over the top and fantastical. When Dick finally leaves prison, he tells a social worker that his "drug habit is a disease like tuberculosis." Soon after being released, Dick injects himself with heroin and dies.

Monkey on the Back, 1956, (National Film Board).

One of the key messages highlighted in *Monkey on the Back* and *Drug Addict* is that the criminal addict and heroin are the sole problems, not the punitive laws and policies that harm individuals and prohibit drug substitution programs (such as methadone and heroin-assisted treatment) and

Dick Smith, depicted as a man who loves heroin more than his wife and children, *Monkey on the Back*, 1956, (National Film Board).

other non-criminal options. The films advocate prison and mandatory psychiatric treatment as solutions to these problems.

Finding legal sources would become even more difficult for people who used illegal drugs. Although, many people who used heroin bought it illegally, some were able to get a prescription for medical conditions.

Dick experiencing withdrawal from heroin following his arrest and imprisonment, *Monkey on the Back*, 1956, (National Film Board).

Cover of *Ciba Symposia*, 1946, (permission from David Malmo-Levine).

Given the criminalized status of street heroin, for over thirty years, the Division of Narcotic Control had attempted to ban legal heroin for medical use. However, some Canadian doctors argued that legal heroin had therapeutic value. Following a recommendation to ban heroin importation by the World Health Organization in 1954, Canada complied in 1955, and licences permitting heroin to be imported were no longer issued. Because Canada lacked a legal heroin manufacturer within its borders, existing stock of the medicine eventually ran out and doctors could no longer prescribe it. A *legal* source of heroin was no longer available to doctors or people dependent on the drug.

Not all doctors and scientists thought criminalized drugs were evil. Some continued to look towards criminalized drugs, such as cannabis, as holding medicinal and spiritual value.

ERNEST WINCH AND THE RANTA REPORT: A HEALTH PERSPECTIVE

The ideas about the criminal addict put forth by the Division of Narcotic Control (DNC, formerly the Narcotic Division), the RCMP, and, to a certain degree, the NFB, were not uncontested. A comprehensive report produced by the Ministry of National Health and Welfare in 1947 challenged the DNC's and the RCMP's stance on criminal addicts and law enforcements' role in drug policy.

Ernest E. Winch also contested federal drug prohibitionist policy.

A Report on Drug Addiction in Canada, 1947

The report highlights that between 1930 and 1946, rather than hardened criminal addicts, "law-breaking by addicts consists mainly of infractions of the narcotic laws" and the majority of convictions at that time were for possession. [4]

From the 1930s until his death in 1957, Winch, Cooperative Commonwealth Federation (CCF) member of B.C.'s provincial legislature, tirelessly argued that Canada should adopt what was referred to in North America as the "British system." This policy included doctors' legal right in Britain to prescribe drugs such as heroin and morphine to people addicted to narcotics. Winch argued that the small group of illegal narcotics users in B.C., who ended up in prison for most of their lives, would benefit from narcotic maintenance treatment.

Ernest E. Winch, CCF member of B.C.'s provincial legislature and tireless activist for people who used criminalized drugs and people with mental health problems, 1943 (City of Vancouver Archives, AM54-S4-Port P681).

ANALYSIS OF PROVINCIAL GAOL REPORTS 1944 – 1953 by E. E. WINCH M.L.A. BURNABY

COMMITMENTS — UP 258%: 2405, 2589, 2570, 3622, 4858, 5091, 6100, 6953, 7159, 8615

RECIDIVISTS — UP 342%: 1131, 1304, 1267, 1998, 2527, 2732, 3318, 3828, 4353, 5221

INTEMPERATE — UP 438%: 1072, 1247, 1338, 2070, 2803, 3076, 4284, 4705, 4911, 5767

DRUG ADDICTS — UP 103%; '54 1/4 136·5%: 227, 224, 199, 293, 313, 345, 400, 454, 462, 392

	OAKALLA	NELSON	KAMLOOPS	PRINCE GEORGE	TOTAL
COMMITMENTS					
'43	1726	129	271	276	2402
'48	3375	229	330	924	4858
'53	5797	404	1092	1208	8615
UP	235%	213%	303%	337%	258%
RECIDIVISTS					
'43	965	38	158	75	1236
'48	1980	70	160	317	2527
'53	3831	183	661	526	5221
UP	297%	381%	318%	600%	322%
INTEMPERATE					
'43	847	24	215	235	1321
'48	1966	143	271	423	2803
'53	3439	370	996	953	5767
UP	306%	1441%	363%	305%	336%
DRUG ADDICTS					
'43	115	2	3	3	123
'48	277	--	-	16	293
'53	417	2	-	43	462
UP	262%	-	-	1333%	275%
POPULATION 1954	14,300	20,500	14,500		

Analysis of prison gaol reports, 1944-53, by Ernest E. Winch (Rare Books & Special Collections and University Archives, University of B.C.).

From the late 1940s to the mid-1950s, Winch wrote to justice and health ministries around the world asking about their drug problems. He also collected data on B.C. prisons and noted the increase in incarceration and recidivism for drug offences from 1944 to 1953.

In 1955, Winch argued before the Senate Proceedings of the Special Committee on the Traffic in Narcotic Drugs in Vancouver for the establishment of *"legalized medical clinics for the treatment of certified chronic drug addicts for the purpose of administering the minimum amount which will enable them to carry on their means of livelihood and refrain from having to resort to underworld sources of drug supply."* Winch also argued that publicly funded treatment and legal narcotic clinics should be made available because many people addicted to drugs *"have no criminal record prior to their addiction...imprisonment does not prevent, nor does it cure, drug addiction."*[5] Other witnesses communicated similar messages to the Senate Committee. Winch also claimed that professional addicts, doctors and pharmacists, had the resources to pay for private sanitariums, had easier access to drugs, and could pay others to obtain drugs for them, if needed. Thus, he argued that the harmful effects of Canadian drug laws were visited primarily on poor and working-class people who were profiled by the police.

A group of diverse professionals in Vancouver also called for a shift in drug policy from a criminal to a health perspective. Headed by Dr. Lawrence Ranta, the Community Chest and Council of Greater

Excerpts from the Ranta Report, 1952

The Federal Government should be urged to modify the Opium and Narcotic Drug Act to permit the provinces to establish narcotic clinics where registered narcotic users could receive their minimum required dosages of the drug.
A variety of narcotic drugs may be extracted from plants. These may be used in a relatively raw state; e.g., opium from the poppy, leaves of the coca plant, or the leaves of Indian hemp (hashish or marihuana). These agents do not present a problem in Canadian communities.
The most dangerous drugs are chemically refined from raw plant narcotic chemicals, or they are completely synthesized from entirely innocent organic chemical sources.[6]

Vancouver's Special Committee on Narcotics set out to study the issue, holding its first meeting in May 1952. The Ranta report, *Drug Addiction in Canada: The Problem and Its Solution*, recommended setting up publicly funded narcotic clinics. The report also argued that the incarceration of addicts would not solve the problems of narcotic addiction or trafficking. Rather, "the addict should be treated as a medical problem," with "definite psychiatric implication."

> **An Authority Speaks Frankly on Narcotics: You can prevent drug addiction – and cure victims of habit** by Dr. G. H. Stevenson
> *The Globe and Mail, February 8, 1955*
>
> Thus, most drug addicts are recruited from the underworld, and most of them have been in trouble with the law before they start on drugs....Secondly, he must have withdrawal treatment in a secure environment, preferably in the psychiatric section of a general hospital.

At that time, the recommendations in the Ranta Report and by Winch for the adoption of narcotic clinics were rejected by the "narcotic expert," Dr. George Stevenson (a well-known psychiatrist at the University of British Columbia who also led the Oakalla Prison Farm study on incarcerated heroin users), the RCMP, and the Federal Government. In fact, Dr. Stevenson publicized his views widely in newspaper articles and editorials, appearing before the Senate Special Committee

> **ARGUMENTS FOR AND AGAINST THE LEGAL SALE OF NARCOTICS** by Dr. G. H. Stevenson
> *Bulletin of the Vancouver Medical Association, January 1955*
>
> He [Ernest Winch] would have addicts get their required supplies through physicians who would be authorized to supply prescriptions for them. That is, of course, a serious debasing of the concept of "medical treatment," as it is the duty of physicians to treat patients in the hope of ameliorating or curing the pathological condition. To ask physicians to be dispensers of narcotic drugs is to ask them to take on the function of the "beverage room" or liquor store"... the proposal for legal sale of narcotics, if adopted, would not only fail to solve the addiction problems but would actually make them more serious than they are at present.

1955 Proceedings of the Special Committee on the Traffic in Narcotic Drugs

The drug addict population, as already pointed out, are primarily criminal, engaged in crime daily apart from the violations of the Opium and Narcotic Drug Act...The Committee notes with interest the evidence of Commissioner Harry J. Anslinger, Commissioner of Narcotics...wherein he pointed out that in areas where low sentences were imposed, the drug problem substantially increased and in areas where there was strict enforcement with heavy sentences the drug problem showed a commensurate decrease....

At the present time there are in Canada 515 medical addicts, 333 professional addicts and 2,364 criminal addicts, totalling 3,212. Of the 2,364 criminal addicts, 1,101 are located in British Columbia....The City of Montreal... has, a total criminal addict population of under 200 and the City of Toronto... under 400.

British Columbia has the largest concentration of drug addicts and, therefore, the greatest problem.[7]

on the Traffic in Narcotic Drugs and speaking on CBC radio. He reiterated that the addict is a criminal addict and narcotic substitution clinics are failures. Stevenson called for the establishment of abstinence-based treatment facilities for criminal addicts.

After hearing from a number of experts across the nation, the 1955 Proceedings of the Special Committee on the Traffic in Narcotic Drugs solidified Canada's prohibitionist stance, reiterating that the establishment of provisions for drug treatment were a provincial responsibility rather than a federal one. Under the leadership of Liberal Prime Minister Louis St. Laurent, the Special Committee also rejected the establishment of narcotic substitution clinics and appeared convinced that the

Prisoners in British Columbia Penitentiary, 1955

In 1955, 24 percent of prisoners (161 out of 663 prisoners) are labelled as "drug addicts." Slightly more than half of the 161 prisoners were convicted for drug possession. Sixty-five percent had been incarcerated before.[8]

false assertion of U.S. moral reformer Harry J. Anslinger, Commissioner of Narcotics, about the value of punitive drug laws was correct. The Special Committee recommended increased and "severe penalties for all traffickers . . . a maximum of life imprisonment."[9]

On CBC in 1960, Dr. Stevenson continued to make his case regarding criminal addicts and addiction:

> People think that addicts, if they could get their drug legally, would work well because they wouldn't have to spend their time out stealing. . . . these addicts we're talking about are really a section of the underworld of Vancouver and of British Columbia and of Canada. They really are addicted criminals . . .
> Even without their drugs, most of these people would still be criminals . . . they're addicted to crime.
>
> — CBC, *God's Own Medicine*, May 29, 1960

Stevenson concluded that "total abstention" was the only viable treatment.

Reflecting on the idea of the criminal addict, Dr. Robert Halliday, Director of the Narcotic Addiction Foundation in Vancouver in 1958, said that the lack of publicly funded drug treatment in Canada following prohibition and the *"absence of community treatment facilities must be directly related to the social concept of the addict as a criminal first, and a sick person second."*[10]

Defying punitive drug prohibitionist policies in the 1950s, such as deportation, reverse onus of proof (meaning drug offenders had to prove their innocence), search and seizure without warrants, writs of assistance (blanket search warrants), punitive prison sentencing (including whipping and hard labour), health and social advocates continued to mobilize in Vancouver. In response to the findings of the Ranta Report and the failure of the Federal Government to acknowledge that addiction is a health issue rather than a criminal justice issue, the Narcotic Addiction Foundation of British Columbia (NAFBC) was established and funded by the Provincial Government in 1955. MLA Ernest E. Winch was one of the new members of the NAFBC Board of Directors.

The NAFBC's purpose was fourfold: research, rehabilitation, treatment and education. However, it was not until 1958 that the NAFBC's community clinic/residence could open in Vancouver. It provided in-patient and out-patient services, including a four-bed residence for voluntary male patients.

In 1959, a twelve-day methadone withdrawal program was initiated at the NAFBC clinic. Doctors prescribed methadone to people who were addicted to illegal opioids such as heroin and decreased their methadone dose everyday. This was the first time that methadone, a synthetic narcotic, was provided as treatment in Canada. In 1963, the NAFBC began experimenting with prolonged methadone treatment.[11] Unfortunately, the efforts of the NAFBC, although tolerated, did not dampen the Federal Government's appetite for punitive drug prohibition. Therefore, as health initiatives and narcotic addiction services began to emerge, punitive drug control continued. This contradiction in Canadian drug policy continues today.

LSD

In the 1950s, lysergic acid diethylamide (LSD) was legal in Canada. Canadian researchers began to conduct ground-breaking work experimenting with the use of this new synthetic drug for the treatment of alcoholism and schizophrenia. In the 1950s and early 1960s, the Saskatchewan Mental Hospital in Weyburn became the site of innovative LSD research. This was made possible through the activism of the CCF, led by Tommy

It was the bicycle trip of a lifetime. In 1943, while isolating pharmacological compounds in plants, chemist Dr. Albert Hofmann accidentally ingested a substance he called lysergic acid diethylamide, or LSD. Puzzled by the intoxication he felt, he deliberately took another dose as an experiment three days later. He then mounted his bicycle and rode into history, experiencing the world's first acid trip.

— Interview with Dr. Albert Hofmann by Michael Enright,
CBC Radio, *As it Happens*, April 15, 1993

Douglas. Under Douglas's leadership, Saskatchewan became the first province to provide publicly funded health care by passing the *Hospital and Insurance Act* in 1947 and the *Saskatchewan Medical Care Insurance Act* in 1961. These Acts made it possible for people in Saskatchewan to receive publicly funded treatment at the hospital in Weyburn. Federal publicly funded health care for all Canadian residents did not come into effect until 1966.[12]

Documentary on LSD, *Hofmann's Potion*, 2002 (National Film Board).

Tommy Douglas had long been interested in health care and mental health. As premier, he set out to entice doctors and medical researchers to Saskatchewan by offering research grants and active participation in new and innovative health reforms and practices. In 1950, Dr. Abram Hoffer took up a position with the Saskatchewan Department of Public Health, and in 1951 Dr. Osmond Humphries came from London to

Saskatchewan Mental Hospital, Weyburn, Saskatchewan (Provincial Archives of Saskatchewan).

Sidney Katz ingesting LSD at Weyburn Hospital, Saskatchewan (*Maclean's*, October 1, 1953, Permission from photographer's son Mike Kesterton).

take up a position at the Saskatchewan Mental Hospital in Weyburn. The two men and their colleagues began to experiment with LSD in the treatment of people with schizophrenia and those labelled alcoholics. Soon their LSD trials led them to support the thesis that mental illness was both biological and social in origin. LSD therapy met both needs because its proponents believed that it triggered new perceptions of the self and was consciousness-raising.

In 1953, journalist Sydney Katz visited the hospital at Weyburn and took LSD under the care of the research scientists there. He documented and sensationalized his visit in a 1953 *Maclean's* article titled, "My 12 hours as a madman."

Earlier in 1953, Dr. Osmond Humphries travelled to California to attend a conference and to meet author Aldous Huxley. Huxley had heard about the experiments with LSD in Weyburn, and he volunteered to be part of the research study. During his California visit, Humphries introduced Huxley to mescaline.

Huxley would go on to write about his experience in his famous 1954 book, *The Doors of Perception*. In written communication between the two men in 1956 about the experience of LSD and mescaline, Osmond coined the term "psychedelic."

Some conservatives romanticize the 1950s as an idyllic decade. However, during the 1940s and 1950s, far-Left and communist organizations were hounded by the Canadian Government. Cooperatives and labour organizations were also viewed as suspect. Yet, by the 1950s, Indigenous people strongly asserted their sovereignty, and political, and cultural rights, and fought against the imposition of discriminatory laws, policies, and the *Indian Act*. Around the world, anti-colonial movements emerged. For African Americans, it was also a time of struggle. The civil rights movement in the United States exposed state-sanctioned violence, institutional racism and Jim Crow laws. So-called beat poets wrote about state-sanctioned destruction, McCarthyism and the violence of Hiroshima. They questioned the "sane" state and the violence erupting from it. They also wrote passionately about altered states of consciousness, mysticism and drug consumption.

At the same time that Huxley and beat poets explored and wrote about drugs and altered states of consciousness, the Native American Church's (NAC) sacred peyote ceremonies were under attack by the Canadian Government. Traditionally found in Mexico, peyote cactus is a

Peyote button (Anne-Katrin Purkiss, Wellcome Images, London)

natural entheogen, and one of its compounds is mescaline. Although peyote ceremonies appeared in Indigenous communities in the southern part of the U.S. in the mid-1800s, the NAC emerged as the central organization for peyote spiritual practice in 1918. By the 1940s, peyote ceremonies were taking place in Canada. However, it was not until the 1950s that a full-blown peyote drug scare emerged in the prairies. Even though the NAC had roughly a few hundred members, some politicians, Indian Agents, and the RCMP sought to have peyote listed as a narcotic drug similar to opium and cocaine. Just like past drug scares, racialized discourses framed the peyote scare. Moral reformers characterized peyote as a dangerous drug used in cult-like environments by Indigenous people, leading to intoxication, addiction and radicalism. In contrast, the NAC sought to "protect peyote as a religious practice,"[13] arguing that peyote contributed to cultural cohesion. Interestingly, the *Indian Act* of 1951, unlike previous versions, promised to "respect Indigenous cultural practices." However, this did not stop the Government from finding other avenues to supress Indigenous cultural practices.

From left: Dr. Duncan Blewett, Frank Takes Gun, William Russell and Dr. Osmond Humphries, October 1956 (Infomart and *Saskatoon Star Phoenix*, photo from Provincial Archives of Saskatchewan).

Following communication with Ernest Nicotine, a local NAC priest, Dr. Osborn and Dr. Hoffer, along with psychologists Dr. Duncan Blewett and Dr. Teddy Weckowixz, were invited to attend a NAC peyote ceremony in Fort Battleford, Saskatchewan, in October 1956 to gather evidence on the safety and the spiritual and cultural significance of peyote. The ceremony was attended by both Indigenous men and women from the Stoney Reserve in Alberta, the Red Pheasant Band in Saskatchewan, Frank Takes Gun, president of the international NAC, and William Russell, president of the Montana NAC. Dr. Osborn writes: "My colleagues and I decided that while they would watch and record the ceremony, I should take part in it, and observe from the inside, as it were."[14] The ceremony began at 8 p.m. and went till dawn. It was documented in the *Saskatoon Star-Phoenix* on October 13, 1956, by Doug Sagi and photographer Gordon Skogland in an article titled "White men witness peyote ritual." The article includes fifteen photos, including images of the tipi that the ceremony took place in, participants sitting in a circle around a wood fire and the passing of tobacco and a cloth sack of peyote. Sagi describes the ceremony as peaceful, accompanied by drumming, prayers and singing throughout the night.

Even though the RCMP, Indian Agents and moral reformers pressured the Federal Government to criminalize peyote, Indigenous leaders were able to counter their efforts, and peyote remains legal in Canada today. Yet, it is still highly regulated. Peyote was scheduled as a drug under the *Food and Drug Act* in 1956, prohibiting its importation, and again in 1958, restricting peyote to medical and clinical use. Interestingly, mescaline, an active compound found in peyote, is illegal, highlighting the contradictory and illusionary drug categories established in the drug schedule.

HOLLYWOOD HOSPITAL

Saskatchewan was not the only place where LSD therapy was taking place in Canada during this period. The private sanitarium Hollywood Sanitarium was founded in 1919 in New Westminster, B.C. Unlike Weyburn Hospital, it was a private hospital that focused solely on the

Hollywood Sanitarium
LIMITED

For the Treatment of

ALCOHOLIC, NERVOUS and PSYCHOPATHIC CASES
Exclusively

Reference: B. C. Medical Association

For Information Apply to

Medical Superintendent, New Westminster, B. C.
or 515 Birks Building, Vancouver

Seymour 4183   **New Westminster 288**

Hollywood Sanitarium, 1925 (New Westminster Museum and Archives).

treatment of people suffering from alcoholism and other addictions. In 1957, Dr. J. Ross MacLean began experimenting with the therapeutic use of LSD and other psychedelic drugs.

According to Dr. MacLean, LSD therapy proved beneficial to patients. In 1959, the sanitarium changed its name to Hollywood Hospital. From 1957 to 1975, more than 800 patients, the majority of whom were treated for alcoholism, received some form of psychedelic drug. However, powerful social and political forces, including fears about the 1960s counterculture movement and the rise of recreational use of LSD by youth, led Dr. MacLean to close Hollywood Hospital in 1975.

The researchers at both Hollywood Hospital and Saskatchewan Mental Hospital in Weyburn were passionate about the therapeutic value of LSD and the subjective experience of their patients. In contrast, under the auspices of the CIA and the Canadian Government, from 1957 to 1964, psychiatrist Dr. Donald Ewan Cameron at the Allen Memorial Institute in Montreal gave vulnerable psychiatric patients LSD without their knowledge or consent in order to "de-pattern" or break down their minds. Cameron claimed that mental illness was caused by patterns of unhealthy behaviours in patients. Cameron's torturous medical experimentations were the antithesis of what the health researchers at Weyburn and Hollywood Hospital strived for.

However, as the 1950s ended, LSD remained legal, and illegal drug use in Canada remained rare. There were only 691 drug convictions in Canada in 1959, and the majority were for heroin possession. Over the previous decades, drugs that were socially accepted became criminal, as did the people who used them. In Canada, the categories of good and bad drugs are not fixed. Consider how the drug tobacco is framed today in

Dr. J. Ross MacLean, Director of the Hollywood Hospital, New Westminster, B.C., 1965 (Permission from Len MacKave and New Westminster Museum and Archives, 726).

comparison to over fifty years ago. Although it is not illegal for adults to buy or possess legal tobacco products, recent public health efforts have inadvertently helped to stigmatize long-term users. Or consider the ups and downs of alcohol in Canada. It has been framed as an acceptable social practice and at other times as an evil to be rooted out. Drugs are not entities with a fixed meaning: our ideas about them are framed by the era we live in.

NOTES

1. Josie, Gordon. 1947. *A Report on Drug Addiction in Canada*. Ottawa: Department of National Health and Welfare.
2. Ibid. p. 36-38.
3. Constable H.F. Price. (1946). "The criminal addict." *Annual Report of the RCMP for the Year Ended March 31, 1946*, 73-82. Ottawa: Edmond Cloutier.
4. Josie, Gordon, 1947.
5. Canada. Parliament. Senate. Special Committee on the Traffic in Narcotic Drugs in Canada. 1955. *Proceedings*. Ottawa: Queen's Printer.
6. Stevenson, George, Lewis Lingley, George Trasov, and Hugh Stansfield. 1956. "Drug addiction in British Columbia: A research survey." Vancouver: University of British Columbia. Appendix A, unpublished manuscript.
7. Canada. Parliament. Senate. Special Committee on the Traffic in Narcotic Drugs in Canada. 1955. *Proceedings*. 663, 667. Ottawa: Queen's Printer.
8. Ibid., 329-331.
9. Ibid., 667.
10. Halliday, Robert. 1963. "Management of the narcotic addict." *British Columbia Medical Journal*, 5(10), 412-414.
11. Paulus, Ingeborg, and Robert Halliday. 1967. "Rehabilitation and the narcotic addict: Results of a comparative methadone withdrawal program." *Canadian Medical Association Journal*, 96: 655–659.
12. This section is partially drawn from the excellent in-depth history of LSD research in Saskatchewan by Erika Dyck, 2012), *Psychedelic Psychiatry: LSD on the Canadian Prairies*. Winnipeg: University of Manitoba Press.
13. Dyck, Ericka E., and Tolly Bradford. 2012. "Peyote on the Prairies: Religion, scientists, and native-newcomer relations in Western Canada." *Journal of Canadian Studies*, 46(1): 28–52.
14. Kahan, Fannie, with Abram Hoffer, Duncan Blewett, Humphry Osmond, and Teodoro Weckowicz. 2016. *A Culture's Catalyst: Historical encounters with peyote and the Native American Church in Canada*. Winnipeg: University of Manitoba Press.

5

Alcohol Prohibition and Tobacco Regulation

Alcohol and tobacco are the most harmful substances in relation to our health. However, more people in Canada use alcohol and tobacco than any other drug. In contrast to alcohol and tobacco, illegal drug use is significantly lower in Canada. For example, about 76 percent of Canadians over the age of fifteen have consumed alcohol in the past year. Only a little more than 1 percent of Canadians have consumed cocaine/crack in the past year.[1]

Today, alcohol and tobacco are legal and regulated rather than criminalized. However, Canadians' ideas about both drugs have changed over time. Efforts to criminalize alcohol for any length of time ultimately failed in Canada because of commercial interests and because it was widely consumed by white citizens from diverse classes, rather than confined to only marginalized or racialized groups. In contrast, early moral reformers linked opium to foreigners, mainly Chinese people.

Contemporary tobacco is thought to be one of the most powerful plant stimulants in the world. Contemporary tobacco is highly toxic and linked to health risks and disease.[2] Surprisingly, unlike other drug treaties, there are no international treaties regulating alcohol, and the global regulations in the Framework Convention on Tobacco Control are weak in comparison to the Single Convention on Narcotic Drugs.[3]

TOBACCO

The tobacco products produced and consumed by most Canadians to-day are quite different than the tobacco grown in North American a couple of centuries ago. *Nicotiana rustica* is the variety of the plant that grew in North America. It is easy to grow and is thought to be one of the earliest forms of agriculture in North America. The plant is considered sacred by many, and some Indigenous nations in North America have long used *nicotiana rustica* for ceremonial purposes. In contrast to later varieties of tobacco, when smoked in a pipe, the smoke of *nicotiana rustica* is not inhaled into the lungs, as it is quite harsh. In ceremonial use, *nicotiana rustica* might be sprinkled onto a burning fire or scattered on the earth. The Huron Nation, for instance, grew and traded *nicotiana rustica* with other Indigenous nations for other goods. However, along with colonization came the loss of fields of *nicotiana rustica*. European traders and settlers favoured commercial grade tobacco, *nicotiana tabacum,* and recreational smoking of the plant became common

Haida pipe, pre-1850
(2934/1, Museum of
Anthropology, University
of British Columbia).

Cree pipe, pre-1910 (William Murison Collection, 2762/42 a-b, Museum of Anthropology, University of British Columbia).

in Europe and Canada. Also, provisions in the *Indian Act* in 1895 to further suppress Indigenous cultural and spiritual practices made it illegal for Indigenous peoples in Canada to sell the plant from their farms. Prohibition did not stop Indigenous peoples from using the plant, even though its use was hidden from outsiders.

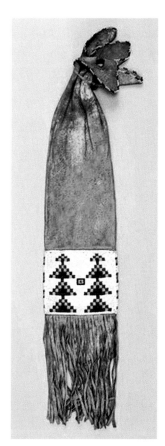

Cree pipe bag, pre-1910 (William Murison Collection, 2762/10, Museum of Anthropology, University of British Columbia.

Formal opening of Macdonald tobacco factory on Ontario Street, Montreal, 1876 (Écomusée du fier monde).

Tobacco growing expanded in Canada in the 1800s in what soon become the provinces of Quebec and Ontario. Both provinces became commercial tobacco growing centres. In 1858, William C. Macdonald opened the first tobacco factory in Canada near Montreal. Macdonald Tobacco became well known for its smoking and chewing tobacco.

Despite its popularity, tobacco was the subject of scorn by some. The Canadian Woman's Christian Temperance Union (WCTU) sought to prohibit the use of tobacco in cigarette form. An 1882 poster by the group lists the harms to youth that they associate with cigarettes: moral depravity, cheating, lying, insanity and loss of manhood.

Tobacco harvesters, 1900–1910 (no. 3642780, Library and Archives Canada).

Even though the WCTU "sounded the alarm" on cigarettes, and despite a private member's bill to ban the manufacture and sale of cigarettes being introduced by a Conservative MP in 1908 in Parliament, tobacco smoking in all its forms was popular in Canada, especially among men. In 1908, the *Tobacco Restraint Act* was passed, which forbade the sale of

Tobacco peddler with cart, Lake Saint John, Quebec, 1925 (no. 3519495, Canadian National Railways, Library and Archives Canada).

SOUND THE ALARM!

Mrs. Stella B. Irvine

SAVE OUR YOUTH!

THE CIGARETTE habit destroys the moral stamina necessary for any line of success.

CIGARETTES UNDERMINE EVERY PRINCIPLE OF MORALITY.

CIGARETTES lead to MORAL DEPRAVITY; LYING, CHEATING, IMPURITY, loss of MORAL COURAGE and MANHOOD and a COMPLETE DROPPING OF LIFE'S STANDARDS.

CIGARETTES introduce the boy to IDLERS and STREET CORNER LOAFERS

CIGARETTES KILL THE FINER INSTINCTS. The CIGARET-SMOKING GIRLS lose the peculiar characteristics of young womanhood which are its charm.

CIGARETTES STRIKE A BLOW AT EVERY VITAL ORGAN. Scientists affirm that "tobacco is the greatest single menace to the health, efficiency and longevity of the race

CIGARETTES UNBALANCE THE MIND. "Many of the most pitiable cases of insanity in our asylums are cigarette fiends."

CIGARETTES STEAL THE BRAINS. High school testimony is, "Memory impaired; clearness of thought hindered; application made more difficult; ambition deadened; the power of will broken."

CIGARETTES GRADUALLY KILL THE POWER OF DECISION. The ability to say "No" is lost

THE VERDICT IS: "CIGARETTE-SMOKERS ARE COMMITTING SUICIDE ON THE INSTALLMENT PLAN."

SOUND THE ALARM!

W.C.T.U. LITERATURE DEPOSITORY,
97 Askin Street   **London, Ont.**

"Sound the Alarm" Tobacco Temperance pamphlet, Canadian Woman's Christian Temperance Union, 1882 (MU 8396.16, F 885-1, Archives Ontario).

Tobacco shop in Midland, Ontario, 1905 (PA-177539, J.W. Bald/ Library and Archives Canada).

cigarettes to anyone under the age of sixteen. A first offence resulted in a reprimand; a second offence resulted in a one-dollar fine. This is quite a contrast to the harsher penalties imposed on youth who violated the *Opium and Drug Act* of 1911. At the same time, the Liberal-led Federal Government under Prime Minister Wilfrid Laurier sought to protect

domestic tobacco growers from foreign competition.

Unlike newly criminalized drugs such as cannabis and cocaine, tobacco products were initially associated with leisure and pleasure, and advertisements were legal and widespread.

Empire Tobacco Advertisement, 1919-38 (1983-27-210, Library and Archives Canada).

Empire Navy Tobacco Exhibition, Sherbrooke, Quebec, 1912 (Topley Studio, PA-012588, Library and Archives Canada).

R.N. Johnston & Company wholesale tobacconist van, Vancouver, B.C., October 30, 1923 (21671, Vancouver Public Library).

Canned Tobacco Typography, advertisement poster (1980-74-7, Artist: Jim Donohue, Library and Archives Canada).

During World War I, the demand for cigarettes grew (in contrast to pipe and chewing tobacco), and soldiers on the front were provided with them. Cigarettes were now commercially produced, legal and popular. Soldiers in World War II also received free cigarettes.

"Send Smokes to Sammy!" "Our Boys in France Tobacco Fund", 1914–1918 (1983-028-3817, Library and Archives Canada).

Today, tobacco products in Canada can be legally purchased by those over eighteen or nineteen years of age. (The provinces and territories stipulate the age limit, hence the age differences across Canada.) Tobacco products are sold in tobacco stores, grocery stores, and newsstands, and they are heavily taxed. Today, there are restrictions on the packaging of tobacco products, and unlike the packaging of Macdonald's cigarettes in the 1950s, graphic health warnings accompany tobacco products in Canada today. The *Tobacco Products Act* of 1997 regulates the sale and production of tobacco products in Canada. Canadian adults can legally grow up to 15 kilograms of tobacco a year for their own personal use. Unlike harsh criminal penalties under the

Delivery of half a million free cigarettes from the Oversea Tobacco League to Canadian Servicemen in the Netherlands, July 3, 1945 (Capt. Jack H. Smith, Canada. Dept. of National Defence, PA-204711, Library and Archives Canada).

CDSA, civil fines are the norm for contravening the *Tobacco Act*. For example, the penalty for selling tobacco to a minor is a fine, not prison time.

Although commercial tobacco is linked to a host of illnesses, diseases and mortality, the drug is legal for adults to consume. The prevalence of tobacco smoking in Canada in 2014 was 15 percent of the population (aged twelve years and older, 5.4 million smokers), the lowest smoking rate ever recorded. Public education, rather than criminalization, is responsible for Canada's decreased smoking rates.

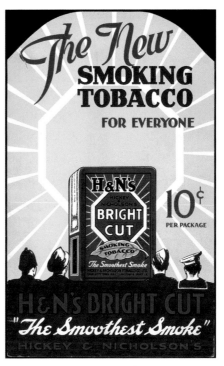

H&N advertisement, 1940 (R1300-26-4-E, Library and Archives Canada).

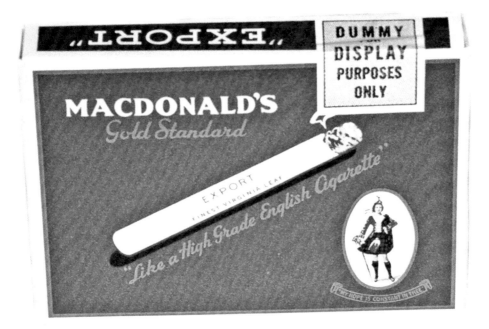

Macdonald's cigarettes, 1950 (Écomusée du fier monde).

ALCOHOL

Earlier colonial legislation that banned the sale and barter of alcohol to Indigenous people, and intoxication, was consolidated under Prime Minister John A. Macdonald, in a provision of the 1876 *Indian Act.* As discussed in Chapter 1, although Indigenous people did not consume alcohol prior to colonization, white settlers did. The first wave of European settlers came from France and Britain and they brought their drug of choice—alcohol—with them.

Prior to industrialization, beer was considered nutritious. It was also

an integral component of social life, especially for Western men. In many European countries, water was often unsafe to drink, especially in towns and cities. It was believed that beer and wine were safer to drink than water in some areas. Ships travelling from Europe to what is now Canada also brought beer and wine for their crew

The Modern Dance of Death: A Sermon in Six Cartoons in Frank Leslie's U.S.-based *Illustrated Newspaper,* 1855–1891 (Library and Archives Canada, no. 1989-406-45 Sources: Molson Portrait Collection, Molson Archives, Montreal, Quebec).

and passengers because clean drinking water was often unavailable during the long voyage.[4] At that time, alcohol was considered to be a medicine, a tonic to prevent disease. When British and French settlers colonized what is now Canada, they brought not just beer and wine, but rum, brandy and whisky.

Wine and beer drinking was not confined to the evening, either. These beverages were consumed at breakfast, lunch and dinner and in the workplace. Alcohol consumption, particularly for men, was an integral part of colonial social life. It is believed that alcohol consumption increased in the 1700s, and some attribute this to the availability of distilled alcohol. One Loyalist travelling in Quebec in 1795 wrote that "a glass of rum and a crust of bread is the usual breakfast of the French Canadians."[5]

Beer and wine were brewed at home. Commercial production began, and small breweries developed slowly, as taverns were established throughout New France, and later the Dominion. In the War of 1812, soldiers were allocated a daily ration of alcohol. Around the same time, new mothers were encouraged to drink in order to aid breastfeeding.[6] Although there were clubs and taverns exclusively for professional and wealthy men, taverns were also social spaces for poor and working-class men to gather in. In the early 1800s, drinking to excess was not frowned upon in the same way that it is today. Many past Canadian politicians were notorious drinkers, including our first prime minister, John A. Macdonald.

In 1832, William Gooderham built a distillery on Toronto Bay. By 1869, Gooderham & Worts was the largest distiller in Canada.

Gooderham & Worts, Ltd., Toronto, Ontario, 1896 (Peter Winkworth Collection of Canadiana, R9266-1617, Library and Archives Canada).

Ontario flyer to end alcohol prohibition (Library and Archives Canada, no. 1983-33-1123 Citizen's Liberty League).

However, not everyone approved of alcohol. In the early 1800s, some temperance advocates wanted distilled alcohol banned. By the mid-to-late 1800s, members of the Canadian temperance movement (such as the Dominion Alliance for the Total Suppression of the Liquor Traffic and the Christian Woman's Temperance Union) sought to have a strong federal law enacted to ban alcoholic beverages across the nation.

The *Canadian Temperance Act*, better known as the *Scott Act*, was enacted in 1878. Similar to the *Dunken Act* of 1864, the *Scott Act* allowed cities and counties across Canada to hold a plebiscite on prohibition. If one-quarter of the electors in the area voted in favour of alcohol prohibition, the retail sale and transportation of alcohol became illegal, except for medicinal, religious and industrial use. In New Brunswick and Ontario, many counties and cities voted for a ban on alcohol. However, many of these bans were short-lived as communities later voted to sell and consume alcohol.

In 1883, the Canadian Woman's Christian Temperance Union formed. White middle- and upper-class women were at the forefront of this movement. They saw alcohol as an evil substance and the root cause

Turner's Liquor Store, 670 Granville Street, 1905 (no. 6714, Vancouver Public Library).

Prohibition petition of the Citizens Committee of One Hundred in an alcohol prohibition parade, Toronto, Ontario, March 8, 1916 (John Boyd, PA-072527, Library and Archives Canada).

of many societal ills such as poverty and domestic violence. The tavern where men gathered socially was depicted as anti-home. The tavern was also framed as conflicting with the needs of industrialization and early capitalism, both of which required well-disciplined workers. Women's public drinking at that time was constructed as immoral and an affront to women's virtue. Christian moral reformers regarded sobriety and self-control as the template for citizenship in the Dominion.

Canadian churches, with mainly white and Protestant members, were also at the forefront of the temperance movement. However, in Canada, the temperance movement was anti-Catholic, anti-French and against Catholic immigrants. Their zealous moralism and ethnic/religious stereotyping offended many Canadians, who also believed that moderate alcohol use was unproblematic.

Public support for temperance waxed and waned in the early 1900s as municipalities and provinces enacted prohibition laws. However, the start of World War I brought about a change in thinking about alcohol. At that time, alcohol prohibition became linked to patriotism and

Police arrest man for illegal possession of alcohol, Toronto, Ontario, 1916 (John Boyd, PA-069901, Library and Archives Canada).

In 1916, Moncton enforcement agents outside their police station emptying illegal alcohol (United Church of Canada Archives, 93.004P/7N).

Liquor still captured by Vancouver Police Department, 1917 (VPD-S214-: CVA 480-215, City of Vancouver Archives).

the war effort. Thus, the temperance movement received a huge boost as Canadians started to perceive the characteristics of a strong nation at war as a sober one. Alongside middle-class Protestant supporters of temperance, some new immigrants pledged to remain sober, and even a few Catholics churches joined the movement. By 1916, the provinces of Manitoba, Nova Scotia, Alberta, and Ontario went dry.

Unlike in the United States, where alcohol was banned from 1920 to 1933, Canada only enacted federal legislation to limit the manufacture and importation of alcohol into provinces where it was already illegal to purchase. In Canada, the provinces regulate sales and consumption, and the Federal Government regulates the production and trading of alcohol.

The federal restrictions were in effect from March 1918 until the end of 1919. Retail businesses that sold alcohol and public drinking establishments (such as pubs, taverns, hotels, and clubs) were banned. Interestingly, unlike drug laws criminalizing opiates and cannabis, private consumption of alcohol remained legal, and in some provinces, domestic wine was not banned. The main focus of prohibition was to curb public drinking. Canadians could still buy alcohol at licensed wholesalers and government-run dispensaries for "medical, mechanical, scientific and sacramental purposes."[7] Therefore, for the twenty-one months that the federal legislation was in effect, many Canadians continued to drink, and others became involved in the illegal production and selling of alcohol. When the Canadian federal ban ended, rum-runners, bootleggers and border-runners were more firmly in place to transport alcohol to dry areas in Canada and the United States for the next thirteen years. Sam Bronfman, a Canadian businessman, also began to engage in the liquor trade during World War I. In 1928, Bronfman consolidated his Montreal distillery with Seagram and Sons in Waterloo. When pro-

B.C. Liquor Control Board Building, 857 Beatty Street, 1921 (no. 10925, Vancouver Public Library).

hibition ended in the U.S. in 1933, Seagram became the most successful exporter of whisky in the world.

Even though federal restrictions on alcohol were short-lived in Canada, several provinces imposed prohibition for longer periods of time. Many municipalities were against the repeal of prohibition because it would end the steady stream of income they accumulated from fines meted out to offenders. Temperance ideology also became more widespread and entrenched in Canada; however, it was far from being universally accepted. Most Canadians believed that moderate drinking was possible and pleasurable. Once the federal ban was lifted in 1919 and the provinces opted to end prohibition, provincial governments (except for Quebec, which had much less restrictive legislation and allowed private grocers and businesses to sell beer, and Alberta, which allowed beer parlours to be opened before other provinces) imposed strict regulations on the sale of alcohol, including the establishment of government-run retail stores and liquor control boards, followed by the opening of beer parlours. However, Prince Edward Island held on to prohibition right up until 1948. It wasn't until 1964 that beer parlours could open there.

The temperance movement and prohibition changed Canadians' relationship with alcohol. For example government liquor stores could not display their products, and pubs had to be inside hotels. But it was not a criminalized drug. Until the early 1970s, when provinces lessened public drinking restrictions, including the legal age, drinking in most parts of Canada was less accepted than in the pre-prohibition era, and the Canadian Woman's Christian Temperance Union remained active.

Alcohol prohibition in Canada had several negative impacts. Most significantly, it led to much police corruption, less respect for laws, and the illegal trade flourished during provincial and federal prohibition. Entrepreneurs illegally transported alcohol to dry areas in Canada and to the U.S. During prohibition, there was a dramatic increase in the number of illegal alcohol stills and the production of unregulated alcohol products, some of which were quite deadly. For example, some bootleggers sold products contaminated with substances that led to temporary and permanent paralysis, blindness and death. The national paper, *The Globe*, recounts many deadly incidents in 1926 in Ontario, one year before alcohol could be legally purchased in government stores.

In fact, rum-running and border-crossing became a viable occupation for many Canadians, especially in economically depressed areas such as the Maritimes. Some Canadians also set up places to consume illegal alcohol in homes, hotels and boarding houses. Although a minority, many widowed women with dependants sold alcohol to locals in order to provide for their families.

Just as importantly, Canada chose to legally regulate alcohol instead

Prohibition Display Booth at the Canadian Exhibition, Toronto, Ontario, 1945
(F-885-8, Archives of Ontario).

of criminalizing it, even though it is associated with more health and social related harms than other criminalized drugs such as opium and cocaine.[8] For example, in B.C., violations of the *Liquor Control and Licensing Act*, such as serving or selling alcohol to a minor, most often result in tickets or fines. Canadians today are not universally accepting of alcohol. Morality still shapes our attitudes towards the drug — there are still dry communities in provinces and territories that ban the sale of alcohol. However, Canada's history with the drug, the social acceptance of moderate and pleasurable use, the negative impact of prohibition, commercial interests, and people's readiness to ignore the laws in order to continue drinking during prohibition and (for some) to participate in the illegal trade, led to legal regulation, taxation and public education, rather than prohibition.

NOTES

1. Statistics Canada. 2014. Smoking, 2014: http://www.statcan.gc.ca/pub/82-625-x2015001 article/141-eng.htm.
2. Weil, Andrew, and Winifred Rosen. 1983/1993. *From Chocolate to Morphine*. New York: Houghton Mifflin Company.
3. Room, Robin, and Peter Reuter. 2012. How well do international drug conventions protect public health?" *The Lancet*, 379: 84–91.
4. Heron, Craig. 2003. *Booze: A Distilled History*. Toronto: Between the Lines.
5. Ibid. 31.
6. Francis, Daniel. 2014. *Closing Time: Prohibition, Rum-Runners, and Border Wars*. Vancouver: Douglas & McIntyre.
7. Heron, 181.
8. Nutt, David, Leslie King, and Lawrence Phillips. 2010. "Drug harms in the UK: A multicriteria decision analysis." *The Lancet* 376, 9752: 1558–65.

6

The Counterculture Movement:
The 1960s and 1970s

In 1961, Canada enacted the *Narcotic Control Act*. The Act was one of the harshest drug laws in any Western nation. It is distinguished by its legal discrimination and punitive penalties, such as life imprisonment for drug trafficking and seven years imprisonment for possession. The Act, however, also allowed for the provision of methadone for people dependent on narcotics under a doctor's care.

In 1961, Canada and other United Nations members also agreed to limit their sovereign control of domestic drug policy by signing the Single Convention on Narcotic Drugs. The Single Convention further entrenched a criminalization approach to drug use and drug policy. In accordance with the Single Convention, the International Narcotics Control Board (INCB), established in 1968, was given a quasi-judicial role in monitoring nations' compliance with the treaties and publishes an annual report on this compliance. As well, the World Health Organization (WHO) was established to review the scientific literature in

1961 Single Convention on Narcotic Drugs

On March 13, 1961, Canada along with other nations agreed to the adoption of a single convention on narcotic drugs to replace other existing multilateral and international drug control treaties. The Single Convention on Narcotic Drugs required nations to criminalize the non-medical use of cannabis, cocaine and opiates.

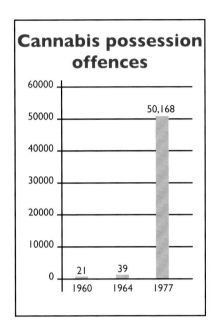

Cannabis possession offences

relation to drug scheduling.

At the same time that the INCB was established, and building on the political and cultural views of the beat writers and civil rights activists of the 1950s, the 1960s were a time of economic growth, the beginning of the welfare state, and social and political turmoil in Canada and other Western nations. The 60s are often described as an era of sex, drugs and rock 'n' roll, but this narrow depiction ignores the incredible political and social activism of the era. In response to the conservative leadership of John Diefenbaker (1957 to 1963), a counterculture that defied conventional notions of politics, human rights, the environment, the workplace, family, sexuality, race, gender, rational consciousness and drug use grew. This counterculture was a challenge to authority, the capitalist state and war, and it was influenced by anti-colonial and liberation movements, the Quiet Revolution, Indigenous activism, Black power, the new Left, student mobilization and women's liberation and the fight for reproductive rights. Communal and cooperative

Rochdale College Council, Toronto. Four members of Rochdale College Council – from left, president John Bradford, Jack Jones, Wilfrid Pelletier and Paul Evitts, November 12, 1969 (John McNeil / *Globe and Mail*).

Rochdale College alternative education and cooperative housing, Toronto, 1970 (*Toronto Star*, photographer: Dick Darrell, Getty Images 502813455).

homes and alternative workplaces sprung up across Canada. Youth and the not-so-youthful came together to demand change.

Opening in 1968, Rochdale College in Toronto was Canada's first free university. Rochdale was a student-run alternative education and cooperative living space. In and outside of Roshdale it was also a time of experimentation with music, art, drugs and alternative consciousness. Cannabis was soon to become the illegal drug of choice for 60s youth. Liberal Prime Minister Pierre Trudeau was elected in 1968, and for many Canadians (although not all) he represented the younger generation. In the late 1960s, university students across Canada called for the legalization of cannabis. In October 1969, 5,500 students and professors from University of Toronto and York University signed a petition calling for the legalization of cannabis. A student-led referendum conducted the following year resulted in sixteen universities approving the legalization of cannabis.[1]

Psychedelic music poster created by Bob Masse for an event at Vancouver's The Afterthought club on 4th Avenue in 1967. Popular Canadian band The Collectors and the U.S. band Steve Miller Blues Band performed (permission from artist Bob Masse, www.bmasse.com).

Poster created for an event at Dante's Inferno on Davie Street in Vancouver in 1967 (permission from artist Bob Masse, www.bmasse.com).

Addiction Research Foundation opens an eighty-bed unit, April 5, 1971 (*Toronto Star*, Getty Images, Frank Lennon photo, 502836647).

Prior to the 1960s, drug control and police attention in Canada was most often directed at racialized and poor people, first Chinese men who smoked opium, then a small group of white poor and working-class heroin users in Montreal, Toronto and Vancouver. A radical shift occurred in the late 1960s and early 1970s when white middle-class youth took up cannabis smoking and soon became the target of police attention. In the early 1960s, there were very few arrests for cannabis possession: 21 in 1960 and only 39 in 1964. By 1972, arrests for cannabis possession had risen to 10,695, and by 1977 cannabis possession arrests had risen to 50,168. Stemming from concern about their children being arrested and sentenced to prison for cannabis possession, for the first time in Canadian drug prohibition history, a significant group of white middle-class parents questioned cannabis control and police profiling of cannabis users. Mainstream magazines such as *Chatelaine*, *Life* and *Time* wrote about marijuana and youth and the harsh prison time meted out to white middle-class youth for cannabis possession. Most youth arrested for cannabis possession did not have any prior arrests — they were otherwise law-abiding citizens who liked marijuana, just like the Chinese men who smoked opium in the early 1900s.

The first meeting of the board for the newly established Alcohol Research Foundation of Ontario met in February 1951. Their offices were located at 28 Avenue Road in Toronto. The mandate of the Foundation changed over the years from a primary focus on research and treatment on alcohol to other legal and illegal substances such as cannabis, heroin and LSD. Later they changed their name to the Addiction Research Foundation of Ontario. As early as 1963, the Foundation's Narcotic Addiction Unit provided treatment for people addicted to heroin. In 1970, the Clinic began a formal clinical methadone program modelled after the program directed by scientists Vincent Dole and Marie Nyswander in New York. The Addiction Research Foundation of Ontario merged

Cinecity's high time over High

The Ontario Board of Censors stopped a private press screening of a Larry Kent's film *High* yesterday eight minutes after it began and sized the licences of both the projectionist and the Cinecity theater.

— *Globe and Mail*, January 17, 1968

The two main characters in Larry Kent's film *High*, 1967 (Photofest).

into the Centre for Addiction and Mental Health (CAMH) in 1998.

Across Canada, some filmmakers also challenged conservative norms of the time. In the 1960s, provincial censorship boards banned depictions of illegal drugs in films. In 1968, the film *High* shook up provincial film censorship boards due to its explicit scenes of young adults engaging in sex, drugs and murder. *High*, set in Montreal and directed by independent filmmaker Larry Kent, was censored across Canada for exceeding "community standards." *High* was not shown again to the public again until 2003.

Georgia Straight, 1969, March 28 – April 3), (permission from *Georgia Straight*, David Malmo-Levine).

On the west coast, Vancouver's *Georgia Straight*, a political bi-weekly alternative paper was established in 1967. Vancouver Mayor Tom Campbell targeted the paper throughout his time in office. The *Georgia Straight* office was raided constantly, and the editor, Dan McLeod, was arrested for obscenity and beaten by the police. Today the paper boasts that it had been charged under Canada's archaic obscenity laws more than any other newspaper at that time. In the 1960s and 70s, the journalists at the *Georgia Straight* took the city's politicians to task and advocated for an end to cannabis prohibition and blatant police brutality against counterculture youth.

Music and cultural festivals were also a key part of the counterculture. They happened together across Canada. The Mariposa Folk Festival in Orillia, the Human Be-in in Vancouver's Stanley Park (later renamed the Easter Be-in), the Toronto Rock and Roll Revival, Strawberry Fields in Ontario and the Man-Pop Festival

CANNABIS —— OUR OBJECTIVE IS CLEAR: TO BRING ABOUT A SITUATION IN WHICH IT IS EXTREMELY UNLIKELY THAT ANYONE WILL GO TO PRISON FOR AN OFFENSE INVOLVING ONLY POSSESSION FOR PERSONAL USE OR FOR SUPPLY ON A VERY LIMITED SCALE

in Manitoba are some notable examples. All of these (and other) festivals created counterculture spaces where the scent of marijuana was common and the likelihood of arrest was less due to the large numbers of people.

Easter Be-In, April 22, 1973, Stanley Park, Vancouver, B.C. (permission from photographer Henri Robideau).

From 1967 to 1972, Vancouver Mayor Tom Campbell loudly protested against counterculture gatherings, yippies, the Liberation Front, and hippies. He called these youth "scum community" and "lazy louts" who could "destroy Canada… and destroy the world." "Tom Terrific," as Campbell was known then, wanted to clean up Gastown, an old neighbourhood in the heart of downtown Vancouver, where, as he argued, these "first class troublemakers" congregated.[2] The mayor was also intent on closing down the *Georgia Straight*.

In 1971, ongoing concerns about the City of Vancouver's police brutality, crackdowns, marijuana arrests and an undercover sweep called "Operation Dustpan" (in response to mayor Tom Terrific's hyperbole at that time) led to numerous articles about police repression in the

Georgia Straight and to the organization of a public event. Youth groups organized a Gastown Smoke-In & Street Jamboree on August 7, 1971. The peaceful gathering was publicized in the *Georgia Straight*. The Gastown Smoke-In & Street Jamboree had two objectives: an end to police brutality and an end to cannabis prohibition.

As Vancouver citizens gathered at the corner of Carroll and Water Streets for the Jamboree, the Vancouver Police Department arrived with dogs, horses and batons. The police charged into the peaceful crowd, swinging their batons, arresting people and creating mayhem as the peaceful crowd attempted to protect themselves. A later inquiry into the event ruled that the Vancouver Police Department caused a riot.

A peaceful crowd gathers at the Gastown Smoke-In & Street Jamboree, Water and Carrall Streets, Vancouver, August 7, 1971 (Glenn Baglo, *Vancouver Sun*).

●HOW TO SHOP AT A SUPERMARKET
● MUD FLATS PEOPLE

25¢ *Vol. 5 No. 189* **TWO ISSUES PER WEEK** **TUESDAY - THURSDAY** *Aug. 3-6, 1971*

GASTOWN SMOKE-IN & STREET JAMBOREE

* * Support the victims of OPERATION DUSTPAN
(109 psychedelic busts in the last 10 days)

* * Bring the means to make wild and incredible music

* * See a giant 10' joint

* * Legalize yourself — free Ga$$town

SATURDAY NIGHT 8:30
MAPLE TREE SQUARE (WATER & CARRALL)

Georgia Straight, Aug. 3-6, 1971 (front page masthead and back page combined, permission from *Georgia Straight*, images from David Malmo-Levine).

Vancouver Police prepare to charge into the Gastown Smoke-In & Street Jamboree, August 7, 1971
(Glenn Baglo, *Vancouver Sun*).

Whereas the police and RCMP were busy arresting young people for marijuana possession throughout Canada, the Federal Government was growing their own in Ottawa for research purposes. Researchers were interested in exploring the health and social impact of cannabis use. For example, the Addiction Research Foundation in Toronto conducted several provincially funded studies on cannabis, including one in 1972 involving twenty young women who stayed in a Toronto hospital for ninety-eight days! Half of the women were given federally issued cannabis each night in increasingly more potent doses. The participants had their kidney, liver and brain functions tested and their behaviour recorded. The women were tasked with weaving colourful belts so that the researchers could also measure their productivity while under the influence of cannabis.

Mayhem at the Gastown Smoke-In & Street Jamboree, Vancouver, August 7, 1971
(Glenn Baglo, *Vancouver Sun*).

The final day of harvest at an experimental marijuana plot, Ottawa, October 1, 1971. The marijuana plants grew as high as ten feet during the summer, and according to Dr. A.B. Morrison of the food and drug directorate, the government-grown grass was three times stronger than street quality marijuana (The Canadian Press/Peter Bregg).

THE LE DAIN COMMISSION

Responding to the rapidly shifting counterculture phenomena, increased rates of illegal drug use and rising drug-related arrests for youth, in 1969, a clause was added to the *Narcotic Control Act* to allow a summary conviction and lesser penalties for possession of cannabis convictions. On May 29, 1969, the Federal Government, under the leadership of Prime Minister Pierre Trudeau, also established the

Canadian Commission of Inquiry into the Non-Medical Use of Drugs, more commonly referred to as the Le Dain Commission, named after the commission's chairman, Gerald Le Dain. Representatives from the Commission travelled across Canada and heard from diverse groups of people who gave testimony about drug use, drug treatment and drug laws. The Commission released their findings in a number of reports, recommending that criminal sanctions against illegal drug users be reduced, the offence of possession of cannabis be repealed and penalties for all other cannabis offences be reduced. They also recommended that medical treatment for people addicted to opioids was needed rather than criminal sanctions. In

Time, 1970 (*Time*).

her dissenting opinion, criminologist Marie-Andrée Bertrand argued for the legalization and regulation of cannabis and its removal from the *Narcotic Control Act*. Unfortunately, her recommendations were not taken up at that time.

Marie-Andrée Bertrand was a trailblazer who helped Canadians understand more fully the harms of prohibition and offered alternative approaches. As a professor at the School of Criminology at the Université de Montréal, feminist, anti-prohibitionist and penal abolitionist, she exemplified the best of scholarly activism. Following her work on the Le Dain Commission, Bertrand continued to push for an end to drug prohibition and would became the president of the International Anti-prohibitionist League, which was founded in 1989.

In 1972, judges were finally allowed to discharge first-time cannabis offenders. Unfortunately though, an absolute discharge was only granted to about 10 percent of people charged with cannabis possession in the 1970s.

PHARMACEUTICAL DRUGS

In many ways, law enforcement and parental and government fears about illegal drugs made the introduction of new pharmaceutical drugs in the early 1960s less visible. In the late 1960s, there were only 300 prescription drugs available to consumers (compared to 10,000 today). New drugs ushered in different ways of thinking and shifted perceptions and practices about prescribing drugs to deal with a wide range of everyday life issues. Drugs like Librium, Valium and Seconal made their way into popular culture and were used for more than therapeutic purposes. Although the Le Dain Commission examined barbiturates, minor tranquillizers and stimulants, the focus of most media reports highlighted criminalized drugs.

Actor Patty Duke reaching for an imagined bottle of Seconal in the film adaption of *Valley of the Dolls*, 1967 (Photofest).

In the Valley of the Dolls, it's instant turn-on...dolls to put you to sleep at night, kick you awake in the morning, make life seem great—instant love, instant excitement... ultimate hell!

Valley of the Dolls

THE MOTION PICTURE THAT SHOWS WHAT AMERICA'S ALL TIME #1 BEST SELLER FIRST PUT INTO WORDS!

20th CENTURY-FOX Presents
A MARK ROBSON · DAVID WEISBART PRODUCTION
STARRING
BARBARA PARKINS · PATTY DUKE · PAUL BURKE · SHARON TATE · TONY SCOTTI · LEE GRANT GUEST STARS JOEY BISHOP · GEORGE JESSEL
SUSAN HAYWARD as Helen Lawson

SUGGESTED FOR MATURE AUDIENCES

Produced by DAVID WEISBART Directed by MARK ROBSON Screenplay by HELEN DEUTSCH and DOROTHY KINGSLEY Songs by DORY and ANDRE PREVIN
Based on a Book by JACQUELINE SUSANN DIONNE WARWICK sings "Valley of the Dolls" theme PANAVISION® COLOR by DeLUXE ORIGINAL SOUND TRACK ALBUM AVAILABLE ON 20th CENTURY-FOX RECORDS

Valley of the Dolls film poster, 1967 (Photofest).

However, popular culture reflected more predominately these shifts in pharmaceutical use. Jacqueline Susann's novel *Valley of the Dolls* became a bestseller in 1966. The novel captures the lives of three young professional white women in New York City over two decades and the phenomena of pharmaceutical drug use such as Milltown, Valium, Dexedrine and Seconal.

Popular culture often emphasized that the line separating legal and illegal drugs is illusionary and unstable. Canadians consumed both legal and illegal drugs, often in ways not recommended by their doctors. In addition, legal drugs were (and continue to be) available and sold on the illegal market.

In an attempt to regulate the illegal trade and production of a grow-

1971 Convention on Psychotropic Substances

Canada signs the 1971 United Nations Convention on Psychotropic Substances. The Convention extended the Single Convention on Narcotic Drugs to include synthetic drugs, such as amphetamines, benzodiazepines, opioids, lysergic acid diethylamide (LSD). The scheduling of drugs under the Convention "assumes a scientific explanation."[3]

UN International Regulatory Systems

The United Nations Commission on Narcotic Drugs oversees drug issues operating under the UN Economic and Social Council. The UN Office on Drugs and Crime is a special UN agency that operates as a secretariat for the Commission on Narcotic Drugs. Every year they publish a World Drug Report. The International Narcotics Control Board (INCB) is comprised of thirteen experts elected by the UN Economic and Social Council. The quasi-judicial, secretive INCB oversees the operation of the international treaties and management of access to medicines controlled by the treaties. Since 1968, the World Health Organization (WHO) is delegated to provide medical and scientific evidence regarding what drugs will be under international control; however, the Commission on Narcotic Drugs makes the final decision.[4] Cannabis has never been fully reviewed by WHO, although a "pre-review" report was prepared in 2016. Prior to that, the last time cannabis was reviewed was under the League of Nations in 1935.[5]

Although Rochdale residents founded a number of alternative and cultural organizations in Canada, the press eventually labeled the College a "drug distribution warehouse." Article in *Watch Magazine* (1994) about Rochdale experimental college and cooperative housing (1967 to 1975), which was closed by government officials in 1975 (David South, editor of *Watch Magazine*).

ing list of "synthetic drugs," the United Nations extended the Single Convention on Narcotic Drugs to control synthetic drugs in 1971.

In 1970, John Munro, the Minister of Health and Welfare declared that the Federal Government would "legalize marijuana."[6] Still, the Federal Government did not fully implement the recommendations put forth by the Le Dain Commission. In 1974, Bill S-19, designed to reform cannabis regulation, was tabled by the Government. If the Bill had passed, it would have moved cannabis regulation from the *Narcotic Control Act* to the less punitive *Food and Drugs Act*. The RCMP and the Department of Justice saw cannabis criminalization as key to Can-

124

ada's drug control strategy. Therefore, they lobbied the public and the Government to reject the Le Dain Commission's recommendations on cannabis reform and Bill-S19; thus, contributing to the Bill's defeat.[7]

Responding to rising cannabis arrests, the National Organization for the Reform of Marijuana Laws (NORML) was established in Canada in 1978. NORML is a national, non-profit group that asserts that cannabis civil and criminal law is both costly and harmful to Canadian society.

Whereas, Canadian society appeared to be on the brink of cannabis decriminalization in the late 1970s, both medical professionals and law enforcement treated people who used illegal drugs such as heroin severely. The *Narcotic Control Act* of 1961 allowed for methadone maintenance treatment. However, following the Act, methadone maintenance treatment was rarely available outside of large cities, and abstinence-based treatment remained the preferred response. In the 1970s, methadone programs were also characterized by rigid and punitive rules, and patients were oftentimes treated like criminals.

Munro won't let heroin be used as treatment
Globe and Mail, March 23, 1972

OTTAWA – Federal Health Minister John Munro has decided against allowing the experimental use of heroin in Canada for treating heron addicts—an experiment suggested in the recent report on drug treatment. Mr. Munro said outside the Commons yesterday that the suggestion for legal use of heroin was "so carefully hedged" by the commission that he didn't think it should be tried in Canada.

Rather than provide less stigmatizing methadone maintenance programs, or better yet, heroin treatment, in 1978, the *Heroin Treatment Act* came into force in B.C. The Act allowed for the involuntary detainment for three years for those judged to be in need of treatment and who were without criminal charges. Those judged to be "addicted" could also be detained multiple times. Brenda Ruth Schneider challenged the Act on behalf of herself and others in B.C. Although never implemented, the Supreme Court of Canada upheld the Act in *Schneider v. the*

1979
Total Drug offences: **64,923**
Cannabis Possession offences: **47,439** (**73** percent of all charges)

Queen (1982), ruling that it was medical treatment of drug addiction, thus demonstrating once again that people suspected of using illegal narcotics are not afforded the same human rights as other Canadians.

By the end of the 1970s, some people believed that the spirit of the 1960s era had waned, thanks in part to the federal and provincial attacks on labour, economic stagnation and wage controls. In Toronto, Rochdale College was closed down in 1975. However, other cooperative efforts lasted. Even though some of the political and social changes that took place in the 1960s and 1970s were short lived, others have had long lasting effects in Canada. Activism to decriminalize and/or legalize cannabis had failed in Canada at this time, and drug arrests continued. Both medical professionals and law enforcement treated people suspected of using heroin harshly. However, advocacy to end punitive drug laws continued over the next decades.

NOTES

1. Martel, Marcel. 2006. *Not This Time: Canadians, Public Policy, and the Marijuana Question 1961-1975*. Toronto: University of Toronto Press: 42.
2. CBC Digital Archives 1968. "Vancouver Politicians Averse to Hippies":
   http://www.cbc.ca/archives/entry/vancouver-politicians-averse-to-hippies
3. Curran, H. Valerie, Philip Wiffen, David Nutt, and Willem Scholten. 2016, November. *Cannabis and Cannabis Resin: Pre-Review Report*. London: DrugScience.
4. Room, Robin, and Peter Reuter. 2012. "How well do international drug conventions protect public health?" *The Lancet*, 379: 84-91.
5. Curran et al., 2016.
6. Martel, 2006.
7. Ibid.

7

Resisting the War on Drugs: 1980s–2000s

As Canada entered the 1980s, drug prohibition and abstinence-based drug services continued apace. They were part and parcel of neoliberal economic, social and political policies. Neoliberalism advocated that people look to the private market for all their needs. Just as importantly for drug policy, neoliberals saw individuals as solely responsible for how their lives turn out. As such, governments cut social supports, including welfare benefits, unemployment protection and spending on housing, education and health. These cuts and policies dispropor-tionately impacted poor and working-class communities.

As has often been the case, U.S. events informed the political, social and economic actions in Canada in the 1980s and 1990s. In the fall of 1986, President Ronald Reagan spearheaded a renewed war on drugs in the U.S. by signing a bill to expand law enforcement budgets and approving mandatory minimum pen-

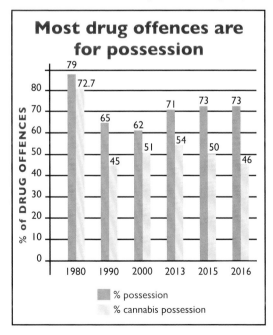

alties for drug offences. Only two days later, Progressive Conservative Prime Minister Brian Mulroney spontaneously announced in a speech that "drug abuse has become an epidemic that undermines our economic as well as our social fabric." There was no evidence to support the Prime Minister's claim; in fact in both the U.S. and Canada, drug use was decreasing by the mid-1980s.[1] Ignoring these facts, the Mulroney Government re-established drug issues in the political arena and installed Canada's first five-year National Drug Strategy in 1987. In 1988, the Government introduced legislation to establish the Canadian Centre on Substance Abuse.

On the international scene, Canada and other United Nations members signed the 1988 Convention Against Illicit Trafficking in Narcotics and Psychotropic Substances. This agreement expanded international efforts to suppress markets for illicit drugs and to criminalize a growing list of legal chemicals used to create illegal drugs.

In 1992, the reduction of harm was included in Canada's Drug Strategy; however, the majority of funds went to abstinence-based programs. After years of debate, the *Controlled Drugs and Substances Act* (CDSA) replaced the *Narcotic Control Act* and parts of the *Food and Drugs Act* in 1997. Unfortunately, the new Act, like its predecessor, remained prohibitionist (e.g., up to life imprisonment for trafficking). A year later, Canada participated in the United Nations General Assembly Special Session on Drugs (UNGASS). The UNGASS slogan was: "A drug free world, we can do it!" Yet, increased drug arrests did not lead to a drug free Canada, and harms increased.

Challenging prohibitionist policies, by the early to mid-1990s two distinct social movements were taking place across Canada. These movements were influenced by effective harm reduction programs in the U.K. and Europe that offered an alternative to prohibitionist approaches. With people who used criminalized drugs at the forefront, the first movement in Canada was a call for harm reduction services. The second was a cannabis legalization movement (described in Chapter 8). These movements continue today; thus, history converges with current events.

HARM REDUCTION

Introduced by people who use drugs, harm reduction practices emerged in the 1980s in the U.K. and the Netherlands as a way to save lives. Harm reduction does not reject abstinence, but it is not the sole objective of services or treatment. Rather, harm reduction advocates assert that non-judgmental and practical integrated services can reduce harms. Many of the harms linked to drugs are not actually specific to the drug: rather, they stem from a lack of legal, unadulterated drugs, and equipment. Drug prohibitionist policies and laws are seen as negatively contributing to and exacerbating the factors that such criminalization claims it will reduce. For example, criminalizing needle distribution negatively impacts HIV/AIDS infection rates.

In defiance of federal law criminalizing drug paraphernalia, and in order to protect people who inject drugs from infectious diseases such as HIV, Alexander Park in Toronto, CACTUS in Montreal and Downtown Eastside Youth Society, Vancouver, opened the first needle exchange programs in Canada between 1987 and 1989.

In the early 1990s, there was a rise in drug overdose deaths, HIV/AIDS and hepatitis C infections in the Downtown Eastside (DTES) of Vancouver. Activists appealed to the City of Vancouver and other levels of government, demanding recognition of the crisis and a change in health and drug policy in order to prevent deaths and infections. Linking these infection rates and deaths to prohibitionist policies, they called for harm reduction services including expanded needle distribution and the opening of an official safer injection site.

In response to the crisis, and the inaction at all levels of government, people who used drugs and supporters set up their own unofficial safer injection sites in Vancouver, such as the Back Alley on Powell Street.

Also, in 1997, the Vancouver Area Network of Drug Users (VANDU), the first drug user union in Canada, emerged in the DTES. Co-founded by Bud Osborn, a poet and social activist, and Ann Livingston, also a long time activist, VANDU advocated for the rights of its members, provided support, and lobbied for safer injection sites (i.e., supervised injection sites).

Vancouver Area Network of Drug Users

(permission from VANDU).

8 a.m. 2 14
9 3 15 SUNDAY 21
10 4 16
11 5 17 (10) October
12 6 18
1 p.m. 7 19 © quo vadis 42nd Week
DOMINANT® 1990

Feb. 12/96

8 a.m. 2 14
9 3 15 WEDNESDAY 24
10 4 16
11 5 17 (10) October
12 6 18
1 p.m. 7 19 © quo vadis 43rd Week
DOMINANT® 1990

Feb 12/96

Lets try to keep track of what we do have from now on eh guys. (Bizzy)

5:45 6 PM alot of running in and out by a few people, IE Taking a smoke, sandwich, coffee and dissappering out the door. I know were're a drop in center but not to be taken advantage of just a smoke and coffee and leave.

6:30 New can of coffee and bag of sugar was bought in by Lenn today lets make it last.

7 PM The body count is 11 everything's going quite well I guess the pamphlet is really causing a lot of enquiry

in certain circle we will be screening for membership through observation of people making use of our wonderful little facility. 9:00 Pm Everything going just fine. Michael came in to see me about working with me as an outpatient I've accepted him he will come and see me two or three times a week. He can also phone me anytime he needs me for help he's quite a nice a guy and definitely needs the help that we offer to those wishing to give up their addiction I now have 6 person that I'm working with I didn't expect

10

Back Alley Journal from poet and social activist Bud Osborn. A journal was kept chronicling the day-to-day running of the unofficial safer injection site, 1996.

The Portland Hotel Society (PHS), a non-profit social, health and housing agency in the DTES (founded in 1991 by Liz Evans, with Mark Townsend, Kerstin Stuerzbecher, Dan Small, and Tom Laviolette) helped to organize many pivotal harm reduction and drug policy events in the DTES, including "The Killing Fields" in the summer of 1997. The protest and memorial was held in the DTES to honour those who had died from overdoses and from HIV/AIDS and to point to institutional and government inaction. The grounds of Oppenheimer Park were covered with wooden crosses bearing the name of each person who had lost their life.

The Killing Fields, DTES, 1997 (permission from photographer Elaine Brière).

Through the efforts of Bud Osborn, PHS and other advocates, the Vancouver-Richmond Health Board finally declared a public health emergency in 1997. Speaking at a press conference in August 1998, Bud Osborn and then-New Democratic Party Member of Parliament Libby Davies spoke again about the overdose crisis and offered concrete solutions: safer injection sites and heroin-assisted treatment so that people who used illegal opioids would no longer be vulnerable. As Libby Davies said: "These deaths are preventable. It's the responsibility of all levels of government to deal with the crisis. We ignore it at our peril."

However, a promised safer injection site did not open, and harm reduction services remained underfunded. So, on July 11, 2000, family members and concerned citizens gathered once again in Oppenheimer Park.

Bud Osborn and Libby Davies, August 12, 1998 (Dick Clark, *The Province*).

Following city-wide consultation in 2001, Drug Policy Coordinator Donald MacPherson authored his report, *A Framework for Action: A Four-Pillar Approach to Drug Problems in Vancouver.* With support from Mayor Philip Owen (and Mayor Larry Campbell in 2002), MacPherson's report was adopted as official policy. MacPherson recommended changes in drug policy, including the opening of safer injection sites and heroin-assisted treatment.

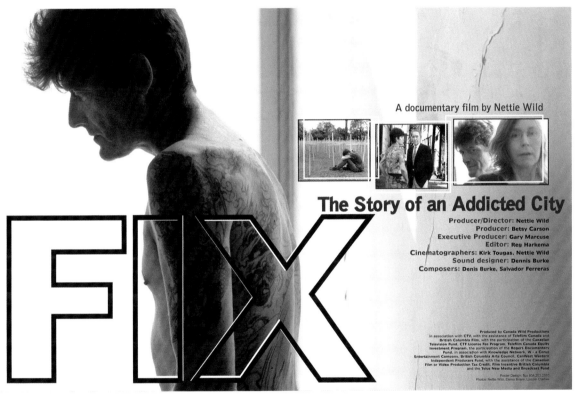

Fix: The Story of an Addicted City, directed by Nettie Wild. The 2002 film captured events leading up to Insite. Wild travelled across Canada and invited audience discussion (permission from Nettie Wild).

In 2003, Canada's first official supervised injection site, Insite, finally opened its doors in the DTES.

Meanwhile in 2002, without federal approval, Dr. Peter Centre, an HIV/AIDS health care facility in Vancouver's west end, integrated a nurse-supervised injection site into its health program and care residence. Federal approval was granted in January 2016.

Small injection room at Dr. Peter Centre (permission from Dr. Peter Centre).

Also, Indigenous women and sex workers increasingly went missing in the DTES and were later found murdered. Indigenous women and their families protested, calling for an end to police inaction and systemic gendered violence stemming from ongoing colonization.

The Gathering. Mural painted for Heart of the City Festival in the DTES, 2016. On May 6, 2014, drug war resister and poet Bud Osborn (in black and white) passed away (permission from artist: Richard Tetrault, photographer: David Cooper)[2]

WOMEN AND HARM REDUCTION

Advocates also sought to set up gender diverse and culturally appropriate services for women and their children. Women who used drugs such as heroin or cocaine were framed as immoral and unfit mothers, and child apprehension was the norm for poor and Indigenous women. Shifts in the 1980s and 1990s in social service and medical regulation, and misinformation about infants born to women suspected of using drugs, led to child apprehension and threats to women's reproductive and human rights in Canada.

Harm reduction services for women were set up in many areas of Canada. Due to the efforts of Dr. Ron Abrahams and others, Fir Square, a harm reduction unit at Women's Hospital in Vancouver, opened its doors in 2003. At Fir Square, pregnant women can stabilize or withdraw from drugs, and nonjudgmental supports are offered, thus enhancing birth outcomes and family stability.

However, many poor and Indigenous families in Canada continue to be torn apart when drug use is suspected.

Motherisk

In 2014 the Ontario Government established an independent review of more than 16,000 individual's hair tests for drugs done between 2005 and 2015 at Motherisk Drug Testing Laboratory at Toronto's Hospital for Sick Children.

The overwhelming majority of hair tests were conducted at the request of Ontario child protection agencies to determine if a parent used drugs or alcohol. Positive hair testing for drugs, including cannabis, was introduced as evidence in court and resulted, in some cases, in temporary and permanent loss of custody of children. However, hair testing for drugs cannot determine frequency of use, dose, if a person is parenting while under the influence, fitness to parent, or whether drug use is problematic, occasional or rare.

The review concluded that the hair testing done at Motherisk was flawed, lacked oversight, and was "inadequate and unreliable for use in child protection and criminal proceedings."[3] Thus, the Motherisk Commission was formed by the Ontario Government to review each individual case in order to determine if the test results from Motherisk were used to remove a child from custody and to assist people whose children were taken into custody or even adopted into other families. Given that women with young children make up the majority of people on social assistance in Ontario, and Indigenous and Black children are over-represented in the child protection system, the Motherisk Commission notes that it is likely that the flawed drug testing disproportionately affected these children and their parents.

POLITICAL BACKLASH

In 2007, Prime Minister Stephen Harper's Conservative-led Federal Government introduced their new National Anti-Drug Strategy that opposed harm reduction approaches and supported law enforcement initiatives.[4] The Federal Government also overturned existing policies, and drawing on longstanding stereotypes and myths to do so, pushed forward many law-and-order crime bills.

The government also waged a war against Insite, spending millions of tax dollars to discredit and close the service. Disregarding research findings on the effectiveness of the service, including the fact that *not one person has died from a drug overdose at Insite*, the government pressed to close it down. In August 2007, a constitutional challenge to the Federal Government's proposal to shut Insite was launched by the Portland Hotel Society and two Insite users, Dean Wilson and Shelly Tomic. In 2011 the Supreme Court of Canada ruled that closing Insite would be a violation of the Charter of Rights and Freedoms.

YOU CAN'T END AIDS UNLESS YOU END THE WAR ON DRUGS.

IT'S DEAD SIMPLE.

THE VIENNA DECLARATION

The Vienna Declaration, 2012 (permission from International Centre for Science in Drug Policy).

> The Vienna Declaration was initiated by the BC Centre for Excellence in HIV/AIDS, the International AIDS Society, and the International Centre for Science in Drug Policy. Supported by international experts, it was officially declared at the XVIII International AIDS Conference held in Vienna in July 2010. The Vienna Declaration states that the criminalisation of illicit drug users is fuelling the HIV epidemic and has resulted in overwhelmingly negative health and social consequences. It calls for a full policy shift and the incorporation of scientific evidence into drug policies.[5]

Still, the Conservative Party's law-and-order mandate continued. For example, in the 2011 federal election, the Saanich-Gulf Island Conservative MP Gary Lunn sent out a flyer to his riding outlining the Party's mandate.

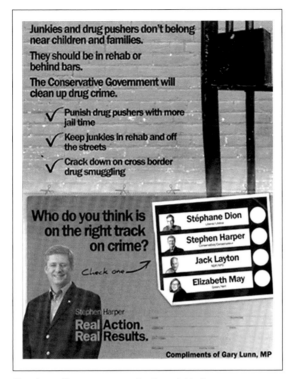

Gary Lunn, Conservative MP, distributed this flyer.
CRG-Government Caucus Services, House of Commons.

Mandatory sentencing really only increases prison populations. Prison time is expensive, not only to tax payers who pay for prison building and maintenance, but also to the people imprisoned, their families and their communities. Prison time does not stop drug use.

Poor, Indigenous and Black people are overwhelmingly over-represented in Canadian prisons. Systemic racism and colonialism shapes disproportionate rates of contact with the criminal justice system.[6] Of the women in prison for a drug charge, many are poor mothers. This reality is in stark contrast to the "pushers and junkies" depicted in the Conservative Party flyer above.

Safe Streets and Communities Act, 2012

- made up of a number of crime initiatives, including changes to the Canadian *Controlled Drugs and Substances Act* (CDSA);
- includes an escalating system of mandatory minimum sentences;
- judges are forced to abide by set penalties for a drug crime regardless of the circumstances;
- and changes to the *Corrections and Conditional Release Act* that increase the length of time in prison for offenders.

The 2016 documentary *The Stairs* sparked discussion in and outside of Canada. It tells the story of people with histories of drug use and harm reduction, working at Regent Park Community Heath Clinic in Toronto (permission from director Hugh Gibson).

VOICES OF PEOPLE
WHO USE ILLEGAL DRUGS

People who use criminalized drugs in Canada have fought to have their human rights protected and their voices heard. Since VANDU was established in 1997, many independently peer-run drug unions have followed suit across Canada (see Appendix B). They provide experiential knowledge, advocacy, education, support, outreach and harm-reduction services. They are leading the way, demanding an end to drug prohibition.

One drug user union, SNAP (SALOME/NAOMI Association of Patients) has been successfully advocating for heroin-assisted treatment (HAT) since 2011. In 2013, Dave Murray, founder of SNAP, and other long time members helped to launch a Charter challenge for HAT.

Drug user group: Western Aboriginal Harm Reduction Society (WAHRS) (permission from WAHRS).

L'Injecteur, a Montreal-based magazine about drug issues published by and for drug users, , established in 2005, May 2017 (permission from L'Injecteur).

Nothing About Us Without Us, made in collaboration with Canadian HIV/AIDS Legal Network, B.C. Centre for Excellence in HIV/AIDS, VANDU, and CACTUS Montréal, 2005 (permission from Canadian HIV/AIDS Legal Network).

Toronto,
National Day of Action,
February 21, 2017
(permission from pho-
tographer
John Bonner).

HEROIN-ASSISTED TREATMENT AND ANOTHER DRUG OVERDOSE CRISIS

After years of advocacy by Dr. Ken Walker, the Federal Government lifted the 1950s ban on approving licences for heroin importation in 1984. Yet, the drug remained near impossible to prescribe due to obstacles and security criteria; thus, the suppliers stopped providing it. Then a heroin-assisted treatment (HAT) trial opened its doors in two locations, Vancouver and Montreal in 2005. Research participants were provided, under supervision, daily doses of legal heroin at a clinic for one year. Similar to international studies, HAT proved to be a safe and effective treatment for long-term illegal opioid users who had not benefited from conventional treatments (e.g., drug substitution treatments such as methadone maintenance).

Unlike other HAT trials, a permanent program was not set up. Therefore, after exiting the trial, research participants were denied the treatment that benefited them. Activism on many fronts led to a different outcome following the second trial (SALOME). A Charter challenge was launched on November 13, 2013, when federal policy was revised, prohibiting special access requests for heroin. Five plaintiffs, Dave Murray, Douglas Lidstrom, Deborah Bartosch, Charles English, and Larry Love (former SALOME participants), and Providence Health Care of B.C., filed a constitutional challenge against the Federal Government in the B.C.

Supreme Court. The case was withdrawn after Health Canada reinstated the former policy in September 2016. As of September 2017, only Crosstown Clinic in Vancouver provides HAT—about one hundred patients have permission for HAT, and plans to expand this number are currently underway.

However, over the last decade, a new drug overdose death has epidemic emerged, this time across Canada, and it has continued into 2017. The crisis stems from prohibition: lack of access to safe, legal, unadulterated drugs, effective opioid maintenance such as HAT, stimulant programs, and safer injection and smoking sites. Fentanyl, a potent opioid also detected in other illegal drugs, has played a part in this overdose epidemic. Ontario, Alberta, and B.C.

Toronto, National Day of Action, February 21, 2017 (permission from photographer John Bonner).

Vancouver, National Day of Action, February 21, 2017 (permission from Canadian Drug Policy Coalition).

have been especially hit hard. In 2016, 443 people in Alberta and 931 people from B.C. died from a drug overdose (with 2017 rates even higher). In Ontario, over 700 people died from overdose in 2015.

In April 2016, the B.C. provincial health officer declared a public health emergency in order to stem the overdose crisis. Lack of action from governments led activists Sarah Blyth, Ann Livingston and Chris Ewart to set up two illegal supervised injection and smoking tents in the DTES in September 2016. Dr. Terry Lake, B.C. Minister of Health, announced in December 2017 that rather than wait for formal federal approval, "overdose prevention sites" (small, peer-involved, informal safer injection sites in community services) would open in Vancouver and other areas of B.C. Although these sites are illegal under federal law, the province supported them because they save lives.

Drug overdose deaths continued across Canada. On February 21, 2017, a National Day of Action on the Overdose Crisis took place across Canada. Supporters gathered, marched and demanded action and an end to prohibition in Edmonton, Halifax, Ottawa, Montreal, Toronto, Vancouver and Victoria.

NOTES

1. See: Erickson, Patricia. 1992. "Recent trends in Canadian drug policy: The decline and resurgence of prohibitionism." *Daedalus*, 121 (3): 239–267.
2. The mural is acrylic on canvas, triptych, 11.5 ft x 22 ft. Image of Bud Osborn, sourced from a photo by Duncan Murdock.
3. Lang, Susan. 2015. *Report of the Motherisk Hair Analysis Independent Review*. Toronto: Ontario Ministry of the Attorney General: 16. https://motheriskcommission.ca/en motherisk-independent-review/
4. DeBeck, Kora, Evan Wood, Julio Montaner, and Thomas Kerr. 2009. "Canada's new federal 'National Anti-Drug Strategy': An audit of reported funding." *International Journal of Drug Policy*, 20: 188-191.
5. The Vienna Declaration: http://www.viennadeclaration.com/the-declaration/
6. Sapers, Howard. 2016. *Annual Report of the Office of the Correctional Investigator, 2015-2016.* Government of Canada: Office of the Correctional Investigator.

8

The Movement to Legalize
Cannabis: 1980s–2017

Although calls for cannabis legalization were not new, by the early to mid-1990s, a social movement was taking place across Canada advocating for cannabis legalization and legal access to medical cannabis. In Vancouver, the movement was spearheaded by Marc Emery, Hilary Black, Dana Larsen, David Malmo-Levine, and others. Marc Emery founded the newsletter *Marijuana & Hemp* in 1994 and *Cannabis Canada* in 1995. He also established Hemp B.C., the Cannabis Café and the B.C. Marijuana Party Bookstore. Marc and fellow activists felt the full force

Marc Emery in front of Hemp BC, "the marijuana & hemp centre for Greater Vancouver," located at 324 West Hastings Street, Vancouver, November 1994 (permission from Marc and Jodie Emery).

of the law as the Vancouver police harassed them and raided their establishments numerous times, resulting in arrests and prison time.

In 1995, the first 4/20 celebration in defiance of cannabis prohibition took place at Victory Square on Hastings Street in Vancouver. Since then, annual 4/20 protests have taken place across Canada in cities such as Montreal, Ottawa, Calgary, Edmonton, Toronto, Vancouver,

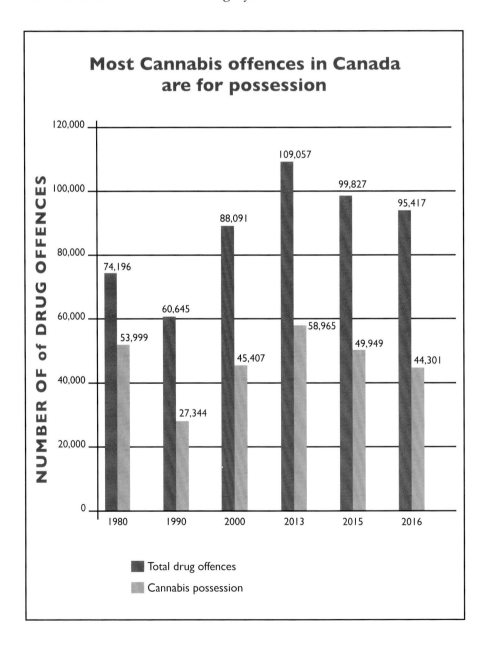

Marijuana & Hemp was written and published on hemp paper by Marc Emery in 1994. Dana Larson was editor. Only one edition of the newsletter was published (permission from Marc and Jodi Emery).

Whitehorse, Iqaluit, Victoria, Saskatoon, Winnipeg, St. John's, Halifax and Charlottetown. The 4/20 message is to celebrate and protest for the legalization of cannabis.

In 1997, the new *Controlled Drugs and Substances Act* (CDSA) moved cannabis from Schedule I to its own category in Schedule II. However, this did not mean that cannabis penalties at that time were necessarily less than Schedule I drugs. Sentencing for cannabis depended on the amount of cannabis found and the category of offence. Critics pointed out that the CDSA sentencing framework for cannabis was at odds with the more lenient sentencing norms that prevailed in most Canadian courts across the nation.

In April 1995, *Marijuana & Hemp* was renamed *Cannabis Canada*, and later *Cannabis Culture* (permission from Marc and Jodie Emery).

Marijuana Activist Marc Emery Extradited to the United States

2005: Marc Emery's business in Vancouver was raided by the U.S. Drug Enforcement Agency (DEA), with the help of the Vancouver Police, for selling cannabis seeds through the Internet to the U.S.

2005: DEA Administrator Karen Tandy says that the "DEA arrest of Marc Scott Emery … is a significant blow not only to the marijuana trafficking trade in the U.S. and Canada, but also to the marijuana legalization movement." Marc Emery's arrest by the DEA was not opposed by the Federal Liberal Government.

2010: Marc Emery is extradited. In Canada he would have been subject to a small fine; in the U.S. he was sentenced to five years in prison.

> **Supreme Court of Canada 2003:**
> ***R v Malmo-Levine; R v Caine, 2003; R v Clay***
>
> **1996:** Police raided cannabis activist David Malmo-Levine's Harm Reduction Club in Vancouver. He was charged with possession of 316 grams for the purposes of trafficking.
> **1993:** Vincent Caine was arrested for possession of 0.5 grams of cannabis in White Rock, B.C.
> **2003:** Caine, Malmo-Levine, and Christopher Clay (Ontario), launch a constitutional challenge to the criminalization of cannabis

COMPASSION CLUBS

Although cannabis use is seen as a pleasurable activity by advocates, it has long been recognized as a medicine, and the plant provides relief from pain and the symptoms of many chronic illnesses. In fact, evidence of the therapeutic benefit of cannabis for the treatment of chronic pain, and symptoms related to a host of diseases and chemotherapy, are well documented.

Part of the cannabis legalization movement was Canada's first medical marijuana compassion club in Vancouver. Compassion clubs (known also as medical cannabis dispensaries) are non-profit organizations, set up to defy laws criminalizing cannabis (and later restrictive medical cannabis regulations), to provide support and alternative health services to patients/members. As well, compassion clubs provide safe, affordable, high-quality cannabis and cannabis products (such as edibles, creams and sprays) for medicinal use.

Lobby of the B.C. Compassion Club Society, Vancouver, 2015 (photo taken by author with permission)

The B.C. Compassion Club Society (BCCCS), Canada's oldest non-profit compassion club, was founded by Hilary Black, Bill Small and Jill Fanthorp in 1997. It is still in operation today. At the BCCCS, members can sit down and talk privately with staff and see the cannabis and herbal products available. The BCCCS also includes a Wellness Centre where patients can learn about other alternative health services, such as herbal medicine, nutrition, acupuncture, massage therapy and counselling. BCCCS and other compassion clubs in Montreal, Toronto, Victoria, Calgary, Halifax and other Canadian cities are not legal under federal law.

Women were at the forefront of the non-profit compassion club movement. The BCCCS was inspired by the Wo/Men's Alliance for Medical Marijuana (WAMM) established in Santa Cruz, California, in 1993. Compassion club staff and volunteers work hard, sacrifice and risk arrest everyday of their work.[1]

Medicinal herbs available to registered patients at the Wellness Centre of the B.C. Compassion Club Society, 2015 (photo taken by author with permission).

In 2014, the B.C. Compassion Club Society conducted a survey of the health conditions of their 5,600-plus registered members. Their findings emphasize that a large percentage of patients have been diagnosed with HIV/AIDS and arthritis and experience chronic pain.

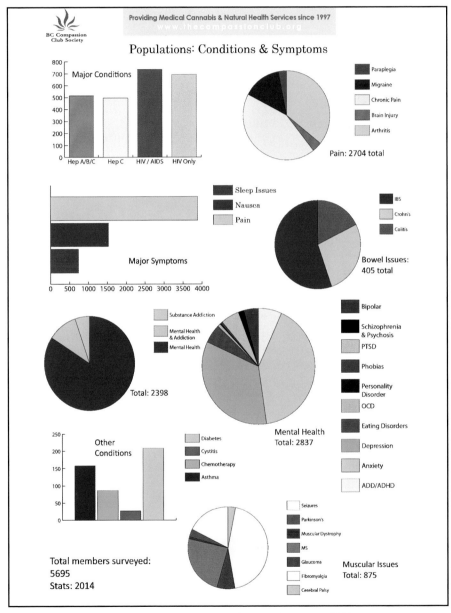

B.C. Compassion Club Society survey of members conditions and symptoms, 2014 (permission from B.C. Compassion Club Society).

CANNABIS AND THE GOVERNMENT

Activism for legal access to medical cannabis also took place in court-rooms. The Government of Canada has been forced to comply with legal decisions (most often Charter challenges) about medical cannabis (due to plaintiffs and lawyers such as John Conroy, Kirk Tousaw, and Alan Young). Responding to the decision in *R v Parker* (2000) that cannabis prohibition is unconstitutional, Health Canada established the Marihuana Medical Access Regulations (MMAR). But the MMAR failed to provide a legal source of marijuana and patients were not allowed to grow their own. In 2003, the Supreme Court of Canada ruled that the MMAR was unconstitutional. In response, Health Canada established an authorized marijuana supplier (Prairie Plant Systems) to provide dried cannabis and seeds for patients.

R v Parker, 2000

In 2000, the Ontario Court of Appeal dealt with Terry Parker, who was charged under the former *Narcotic Control Act* and under the *Canadian Drugs and Substances Act* (CDSA) with cultivation and possession of marihuana [as the Canadian Government spelled "marijuana"]. He needed the marihuana to control his epilepsy. As there was no legal marihuana source, he grew his own.
The Ontario Court of Appeal upheld the trial finding that the CDSA prohibition against marihuana infringed Parker's Charter rights. The Court concluded that forcing Parker to choose between his health and imprisonment violated his right to liberty and security of the person.[2]

At that time, Prairie Plant Systems' one strain of marijuana was grown in an abandoned copper mine in Flin Flon, Manitoba. The company was directed by Health Canada to provide marijuana by courier only. Patients were not allowed to consult with company staff in person. Legal medical marijuana programs exist in twenty-nine U.S. states, and in other countries, but Canada was the first nation to establish a federal medical marijuana program. However, medical cannabis users complained the MMAR application process was excessively long. As well, a medical specialist (rather than a general practitioner) had to support

Federal Health Minister Allan Rock (right) and Brent Zettl, president and CEO of Prairie Plant Systems, inspect the crop, August 2, 2001 (Canadian Press, photo/ Frank Gunn, 2001).

the application for patients who were not terminally ill. Canadian physicians, without their consent, became gatekeepers to the program.

Findings from two separate federal commissions on drugs were released in 2002. The House of Common's report recommended the decriminalization of cannabis.

Led by Senator Pierre Claude Nolan, the Senate Special Committee on Illegal Drugs report, *Cannabis: Our Position for a Canadian Public Policy*, concluded that cannabis prohibition is a failure. It noted that billions of dollars have gone into law enforcement with no great effect on drug use rates and trafficking. The report strongly recommended the legalization of cannabis possession, licensing for producers and retailers, the recognition of the expertise of compassion clubs and improved federal medical cannabis policy.[3]

However, the majority of these recommendations were rejected by the Federal Government. Instead, a drug scare about marijuana growing ("grow ops") gained momentum in the late 1990s and 2000s. With little substantial evidence, the RCMP, local police, media and moral reformers linked both licensed medical and illegal cannabis growing to racialized gangs, organized crime, violence and public safety.

These moral reformers demonized cannabis growing and backed municipal electrical inspections of homes, provincial laws allowing the disclosure of electrical

Senator Pierre Claude Nolan, who advocated for cannabis reform, 2012, Annual NATO Session in Prague (@NATOPA).

Delta police raid Cannabis growing, North Delta, March 6, 2000 (*Vancouver Sun.* Photo by Glenn Baglo).

consumption information and provincial civil forfeiture laws enacted in eight provinces since 2001. These initiatives do not include full protections under criminal law and the Charter and assume guilt rather than innocence. Municipal initiatives allow warrantless entries into homes.

This was all taking place in the context of a panic that was not based on substantial evidence. Supreme Court decisions, scholarly research and a federal Department of Justice study all found that the majority of cannabis grow ops are not linked to organized crime, violence or threats to public safety.[4]

Popular culture also provided alternative narratives. Similar to the comedic films that normalize cannabis use, selling, and growing popularized by Cheech and Chong in the 1970s and 1980s, several films of the era — *Half Baked* (1998), *Harold & Kumar Go to White Castle* (2004), *Growing Op* (2008), and *Trailer Park Boys: The Movie* (2004) — did the same. *Harold and Kumar* is also one of the first films to include a scene about legal medical cannabis.

Harold & Kumar Go to White Castle, 2004 (Photofest).

LEGALIZING CANNABIS

The *Safe Streets and Communities Act* enacted in 2012 also included punitive mandatory minimum sentencing for some cannabis offences, including six months' prison time for growing more than five cannabis plants. Mandatory drug penalties limit judicial discretion and the application of less punitive sentencing. In 2012, Washington and Colorado voted to legalize and regulate cannabis. A person in Colorado could legally grow six cannabis plants; a Canadian could be sentenced to six months in prison for the same activity.

Due to rising cannabis possession arrests in British Columbia (they doubled between 2005 and 2011), and harms stemming from prohibition, cannabis activist Dana Larsen and others created the Sensible B.C. campaign to call for the Provincial Government to pass the *Sensible Po-*

licing Act in 2012. The Act would allow the police to stop arresting people for cannabis possession. Within ninety days in 2013, over 200,000 people signed their petition. Sensible B.C. also continued to rally the Federal Government to legalize cannabis.

Safe Streets and Communities Act, 2012: Cannabis

• Any adult convicted of growing more than five cannabis plants will serve six months in prison
• If the plants were grown close to a school or place where youth congregate, the sentence is one-year in prison
• The maximum penalty for the production of marijuana was increased from seven to fourteen years imprisonment

---

ILLEGAL CANNABIS CONTINUES

Meanwhile, in response to a number of court cases, in 2014 the Federal Government introduced the Marijuana for Medical Purposes Regulation (MMPR) making medical cannabis more accessible. But the new rules did not allow for personal or designated growers, making medical cannabis expensive and inaccessible for those too ill or without the space or expertise to grow for themselves. A Supreme Court ruling in 2016, *Allard et al. v Canada,* upheld the right of authorized patients and designated growers to grow cannabis. Consequently, the new Access to Cannabis for Medical Purposes Regulations (ACMPR) of 2016, allowed personal and designated growers to produce limited amounts.

To date, fifty-eight medical cannabis producers have been approved. All licensed cannabis producers must grow indoors. The authorized cannabis producers can sell to patients only through the mail and courier service, and patients are not allowed on site. Consultation with staff is provided over the phone. The buildings must have secure fencing, reinforced walls and CCTV recording the perimeter and all rooms where cannabis is present, among other security requirements. Thus, it is expensive to gain a licence. Local and small producers, compassion clubs and dispensaries may not have the capital to build the required

Cannabis dispensary, Stressed and Depressed, Vancouver, B.C., 2017 (permission from David Malmo-Levine)

Canna Farmacy, Vancouver, B.C, 2015 (permission from photographer Iain Mitchell-Boyd)

facilities, therefore remaining unauthorized and illegal.

As a result, new illegal dispensaries have sprung up across Canada. The dispensary storefronts are quite diverse: some look like pharmacies or wellness centres, while others adopt more playful names such as Mary Jane's and Cannabis Culture. If they are left outside of the legal market, their expertise about their patients, affordable, good quality and organic cannabis, and knowledge about different strains and their effects may remain lost and unacknowledged by Health Canada.

In 2015, Vancouver created a regulatory framework for "illegal" cannabis dispensaries that drew from activist and cannabis researcher Rielle Capler's self-regulations for cannabis dispensaries, which was created for the Canadian Association of Medical Cannabis Dispensaries. Victoria followed suit, and now dispensaries in both cities must apply for a licence and abide by these regulations regarding licensing fees, security and location. In contrast, in 2016 and 2017, Toronto police raided a number of dispensaries and arrested people owning and working in them.

THE TASK FORCE

Following the federal election in 2015, the Government established a Task Force on marijuana legalization and regulation. The Task Force received submissions from organizations and 28,880 individual online responses. They met with governments and conducted roundtable dis-

A Framework for the Legalization and Regulation of Cannabis in Canada

- Create a separate *Cannabis Control Act*
- Minimum age of purchase: 18
- 30-gram limit for personal possession
- Personal cultivation limited to four plants no higher than 100 cm
- Encourage a diverse, competitive market that includes small producers
- Permit dedicated spaces for consumption outside one's home
- Support a separate medical access framework for patients
- Develop comprehensive education and invest in data collection and research

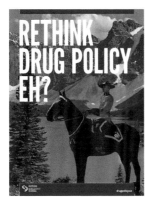

Founded in 2010, Canadian Drug Policy Coalition poster for drug policy reform (permission from Canadian Drug Policy Coalition).

cussions with a diverse range of stakeholders. Their final report was released in December 2016.

Many of the recommendations made by the Task Force were taken up in the proposed *Cannabis Act* introduced to the House of Commons on April 13, 2017. The Act also includes the regulation of cannabis under the ACMPR and the Industrial Hemp Regulations. Rather than breaking fully away from criminalization, some of the penalties for offences under the Act are quite punitive (in contrast to the *Tobacco Act*), including a maximum sentence of up to fourteen years in prison for selling to a minor or growing more than four cannabis plants without authorization. Youth (ages 12–18) can also face criminal penalties if convicted of possessing more than five grams of cannabis. So far, the Government has resisted calls to decriminalize cannabis in advance of legalization or to exonerate people who have criminal records for cannabis offences. This has serious repercussions. In 2016, the year following the Governments' Liberal-led election victory and promise to legalize cannabis, more than 44,000 people were arrested for cannabis possession. Also, it is not clear whether or not local "illegal" dispensaries and small growers will make it into the legal market if cannabis is legalized in 2018.

NOTES

1. Email communication with Rielle Capler, April 4, 2017.
2. Summarized from 2016 Supreme Court of Canada ruling, *Allard et al. v. Canada*, 2016 FC 236, pp. 17-18.
3. Canada, Parliament. 2003. *Cannabis: Report of the Senate Special Committee on Illegal Drugs* abridged version. Senate Special Committee on Illegal Drugs.
4. Boyd, Susan, and Connie Carter, C. 2014. *Killer Weed: Marijuana Grow Ops, Media, and Justice.* Toronto: University of Toronto Press. *Allard et al. v. Canada*, 2016 FC 236; Solecki, André, Kimberly Burnett, and Kuan Li. 2011. "Drug production cases in selected Canadian jurisdictions: A study of case file characteristics 1997–2005." Ottawa: Department of Justice. Released under the Access to Information Act; Capler, Rielle, Neil Boyd, and Donald MacPherson. 2016. *Organized Crime in the Cannabis Market: Evidence and Implications.* Vancouver: Canadian Drug Policy Coalition, 2016. Available at: http://drugpolicy.ca wp-content/uploads/2016/11/CDPC_Submission_Cannabis-and-Organized-Crime_ Aug9-2016_Full-Final.pdf

9

Where to Now?

This book illuminates Canada's history of drug prohibition—its laws, policies and resistance to them—and how it has shaped the lives of millions of Canadians. For over a century, criminalized drugs have been demonized, as were the people who used and sold them. Criminalized drugs have long been linked to marginalized and racialized groups, who have been depicted as outsiders to the nation threatening moral Canadians. Politicians, law enforcement, media and vocal spokespeople fuelled drug scares and circulated fabrications and lurid, exaggerated accounts of drug use and trafficking in support of punitive drug policies. Worn out tropes about people who use and/or sell drugs have promoted social injustice. However, today Canada is at a crossroads. Increasingly, drug prohibition is understood as a social justice and human rights issue.

History, however, is never definitive. Local stories, new discoveries and uncovered material can emerge, illuminating once again the danger of assuming history is static. Over the years, there have been many pivotal moments in Canadian drug prohibition and challenges to it. Community activists, people who use drugs, constitutional lawyers, researchers and service providers have long challenged Canadian prohibitionist policies. Knowing the history of Canadian prohibition can guide us to better understand current events and notions about drugs and the people who use them. Knowing about Canadian drug prohibition allows us to critically reflect on past practices, legal regulation, law enforcement, moral reformers and their agendas, new events and avenues to adopt. The field is wide open because people implement drug prohibition, and people can also dismantle it or change its course. Laws and policies are not static, nor neutral.

For more than a century, drug prohibition has been and continues to be an expensive failure. Our reliance on the criminal law to eliminate illegal drug production, selling and use has not proved effective. In fact, it has only worsened the health and well-being of those who use drugs, and it has also resulted in increased imprisonment, child apprehension and human rights violations. Importantly, criminalization (prohibition) has undermined health services such as harm reduction services and other programs that effectively counter HIV and hepatitis C epidemics and drug overdose deaths. The harms stemming from prohibition are not limited to illegal drug users and traffickers — families and communities also bear the brunt of our drug policies, as do other nations outside our borders such as Mexico and Colombia. For this reason, Mexico and Latin American nations have been critical over the last thirty years of international drug conventions and the devastating damage the Western-driven war on drugs and neoliberal policies have on them. Activists in Canada and around the world are striving to change all this.

International drug control treaties are outdated, inflexible and do not reflect contemporary societal, cultural and public health concerns. In fact, the Canadian *Report of the Senate Special Committee on Illegal Drugs* noted in 2003 that "the international classifications of drugs are arbitrary and do not reflect the level of danger they represent to health or to society." The International Control Board (INCB) has also come under scrutiny. Their lack of dialogue with nations, of accountability and of transparency, and their criticism of policies and public health and harm reduction initiatives have been increasingly questioned by scholars, government officials, drug user unions and national and international drug policy reform groups, such as Canadian Drug Policy Coalition, Canadian HIV/AIDS Legal Network, Global Drug Policy Conservatory, Mexico United Against Crime, Transform Drug Policy Foundation, Transnational Institute, International Centre on Human Rights

Memorial wall for activist poet Bud Osborn, 100 Block East Hastings, Vancouver., May 16, 2014, (permission from Dave Murray).

and Drug Policy, Drug Policy Alliance, and Washington Office on Latin America.

Supporters of punitive drug policies fear that drug use rates will skyrocket if prohibition ends. However, recent history demonstrates that such fears are misguided. In 1976, the Netherlands implemented de facto decriminalization through the *Dutch Opium Act* for the possession and sale of up to 30 grams of cannabis. In order to protect youth and separate them from illegal markets selling "harder" drugs such as opiates and cocaine, cannabis shops (similar to coffee shops) were allowed to be established under strict rules and regulations. Using the most recent drug-use statistics available, cannabis rates have not increased in the Netherlands, and cannabis use is much lower there.[1]

Responding to sharp increases in heroin use, overdose deaths, and HIV/AIDS in the 1980s and 1990s, the decriminalization of personal use and possession of all drugs, not just cannabis, came into force in Portugal in 2001. The move away from criminal sanctions and stigma related to criminalization was part of a much wider social and health public policy strategy in the country. Decriminalization in Portugal co-exists with other measures, such as expanded prevention, treatment, harm reduction services and social supports. Rather than criminalization, pragmatism, humanism and social integration are key to Portugal's drug policy. Since 2001, drug-related deaths and HIV infections have decreased, drug use has decreased for adolescents and those ages 15 to 24, and drug prices have not lowered (as opponents claimed they would).[2]

When Canada established the first federal medical marijuana program in the world, the sky did not fall down. Twenty-nine U.S. states have legal medical marijuana programs. Uruguay became the first nation in the world to end cannabis prohibition in 2014. Eight U.S. states and the District of Columbia also ended cannabis prohibition between 2012 and 2016; 20 percent of Americans now live in states that have legalized and regulated cannabis. The cannabis plant did not change; rather, attitudes about prohibition and the plant changed.

In those states, provinces and nations that have turned away from punitive drug policies, addiction and drug use rates have not increased substantially and youth were not negatively affected. Given Canada's drug overdose death crisis, will all levels of government move quickly to set up more supervised injection sites, heroin assisted treatment, other flexible drug substitution programs and public education as the first steps to saving lives? In order to save lives now, will provinces defy federal law and set up overdose prevention sites that allow smoking, ingestion and injection (as B.C. has done) rather than waiting for federal approval?

Until 2016, Insite stood alone as the only authorized safer injection site in Canada. By May 2017, eight other sites received approval and the application process has become less obstructionist. Health Canada also announced a new process that will allow the importation and use of medications not yet authorized in Canada, such as legal heroin, to help stem the drug overdose crisis. Public health officials can now send a request to Health Canada for bulk quantities (instead of individual special access requests) of the drug so that it can be more efficiently prescribed to those most in need at clinics and other locations. It is too early to know whether long-held prohibitionist attitudes will curtail some public health officials from implementing change.

The Federal Government also passed the *Good Samaritan Drug Overdose Act* in 2017. The Act provides an exemption from criminal charges of simple possession of an illegal drug for anyone who calls 911 for themselves or another person who is overdosing, and for anyone else at the site when emergency help arrives. Yet, people are reluctant to call 911 if they fear that they may be charged with another drug charge, such as possession for the purpose of trafficking.

In order to more fully stem the harms associated with prohibition, including overdose deaths, diverse Canadian groups and individuals have long advocated for an end to drug prohibition and the criminalization of marginalized groups of people, as have international groups. Yet, each group's blueprint to legally regulate currently criminalized drugs differs slightly. Similarly, each U.S. state that voted to legalize cannabis created quite different policies for the production, sale, distribution and possession of the plant. And there are different city initiatives too. For example, in 2017 Oakland City Council in California adopted an Equity Permit Program for medical cannabis production licences. The Program prioritizes those who were unfairly impacted by the U.S. "War on Drugs": long time residents in high arrest areas, racialized and poor people, including people convicted of a cannabis offence. The policy will extend to recreational non-medical cannabis producers in 2018.

On April 13, 2017, the Canadian Government tabled Bill-45, the *Cannabis Act*, to the House of Commons. The Act fails to make a clean break away from prohibition. Unlike tobacco regulation, the *Cannabis Act* includes harsh criminal penalties for some offences. However, changes

Historically, in Canada, the majority of drug arrests have been for possession and young adults and youth experience higher arrest rates for cannabis possession than older Canadians. In 2016, 73 percent of all police-reported drug offences were for possession.

can be made to the Act prior to its enactment. It is also unknown how each province, territory and municipality will take up their responsibilities in relation to cannabis distribution and sale.

The Canadian Government, thus far, has refused to direct law enforcement to stop arresting people for cannabis possession now rather than waiting until the *Cannabis Act* is finally enacted. It is unclear whether small cannabis producers, compassion clubs and dispensaries will be supported by federal and provincial governments to participate in the legal cannabis market if and when the Act is made into law. Will the expertise of medical cannabis and illegal cultivators be recognized in the policy making stage and invited to participate in the legal market set up? Will people who have a criminal record for cannabis possession be exonerated?

Will Canada choose to decriminalize and/or to legally regulate all illegal drugs? Will the Government address the historic violence and injustice of drug prohibition? If so, will Canada be successful in eliminating social structural violence and systemic race, class and gender discrimination against people who used drugs/plants that were criminalized? Or will we create a new regime to continue punishing people? Eventually, these and many other questions will be addressed in Canada. Current events will affect people's experience of drug policy and ultimately, shape history.

NOTES

1. Reinarman, Craig. 2017. "Going Dutch: Drug policy at the crossroads." *Criminology & Public Policy*, 15(3): 885–895.
2. Félix, Sónia, and Pedro Portugal. 2017. "Drug decriminalization and the price of illicit drugs." *International Journal of Drug Policy*, 39, 121-129; Murkin, George. 2014. *Drug Decriminalization in Portugal: Setting the Record Straight*. London: Transform Drug Policy Foundation: 1–4.

APPENDIX A
National and International Drug Reform Organizations

Abortion Rights Coalition Canada: www.arcc-cdac.ca/home.html

Anyone's Child: Families for Safer Drug Control:
    www.anyoneschild.org/about/

Canadian Association of Medical Cannabis Dispensaries:
    www.camcd-acdcm.ca

Canadian Drug Policy Coalition: www.drugpolicy.ca

Canadian Foundation for Drug Policy: www.cfdp.ca

Canadian Harm Reduction Network:
    www.canadianharmreduction.com

Canadian HIV/AIDS Legal Network: www.aidslaw.ca

Canadian Students for Sensible Drug Policy: www.cssdp.org/about/

Cannabis Trade Alliance of Canada: www.sustainablecannabis.ca

CAPUD: www.capud.ca

Drug Policy Alliance: www.drugpolicy.org

Global Drug Commission on Drug Policy:
    www.globalcommissionondrugs.org

International Centre for Science in Drug Policy: www.icsdp.org

International Network of People who Use Drugs (INPUD):
    www.inpud.net/en/links

MAPS Canada: www.mapscanada.org

National Advocates for Pregnant Women:
    www.advocatesforpregnantwomen.org

NORML Canada: www.norml.ca

Pivot Legal Society: www.pivotlegal.org

Moms Stop the Harms: www.momsstoptheharm.com

Transform Drug Policy: www.tdpf.org.uk

Transnational Institute, International Centre on
Human Rights and Drug Policy:
www.tni.org/en/briefing/human-rights-and-drug-policy

Washington Office on Latin America: www.wola.org

APPENDIX B

Drug User Unions

AAWEAR (Alberta Addicts Who Educate and Advocate Responsibly), 2002

AQPSUD (L'Association Québécoise pour la promotion de la santé des personnes utilisatrices de drogues), 2011

B.C/Yukon Association of Drug War Survivors, 2009

BCAPOM (British Columbia Association of People on Methadone), 2001

CAPUD (Canadian Association of People Who Use Drugs), 2012

DUAL (Drug Users Advocacy League, Ottawa), 2010

EIDGE (Eastside Illicit Drinkers Group for Education, Vancouver), 2010

INPUD (International Network of People Who Use Drugs), 2006

MANDU (Manitoba Network of Drug Users)

Méta d'Âme (Association of People who use Opiates, Montreal), 1999

REDUN (Rural Empowered Drug User Network, Nelson, BC 2004 and Grand Forks, BC, 2004)

SNAP (Salome/Naomi Association of Patients, formerly NPA, NAOMI Patients Association, Vancouver), 2011

SOLID (Society of Living Illicit Drug Users, Victoria), 2003

TDUU (Toronto Drug Users Union, Toronto), 2008

UNDUN (Unified Network of Drug Users Nationally), 2002

VANDU (Vancouver Area Network of Drug Users), 1997

WAHRS (Western Aboriginal Harm Reduction Society), 2002 [1]

1. Complied with input from the drug user unions and Canadian Association of People Who Use Drugs (CAPUD). (2014). *Collective Voices, Effecting Change: Final Report of National Meeting of Peer-Run Organizations of People Who Use Drugs*. Victoria, BC: Centre for Addictions Research of British Columbia.

INDEX